MOMENTUM

SOCIOLOGICAL OBSERVATIONS

Series Editor: JOHN M. JOHNSON, *Arizona State University*

"This new series seeks its inspiration primarily from its subject matter and the nature of its observational setting. It draws on all academic disciplines and a wide variety of theoretical and methodological perspectives. The series has a commitment to substantive problems and issues and favors research and analysis which seek to blend actual observations of human actions in daily life with broader theoretical, comparative, and historical perspectives. SOCIOLOGICAL OBSERVATIONS aims to use all of our available intellectual resources to better understand all facets of human experience and the nature of our society."

—*John M. Johnson*

Volumes in this series:

1. THE NUDE BEACH, by Jack D. Douglas and Paul K. Rasmussen, with Carol Ann Flanagan
2. SEEKING SPIRITUAL MEANING, by Joseph Damrell
3. THE SILENT COMMUNITY, by Edward William Delph
4. CROWDS AND RIOTS, by Sam Wright
5. THE MAD GENIUS CONTROVERSY, by George Becker
6. AMATEURS, by Robert A. Stebbins
7. CARETAKERS, by David R. Buckholdt and Jaber F. Gubrium
8. HARD HATS, by Jeffrey W. Riemer
9. LOVE AND COMMITMENT, by Gary Schwartz and Don Merten with Fran Behan and Allyne Rosenthal
10. OUTSIDERS IN A HEARING WORLD, by Paul C. Higgins
11. MOMENTUM, by Peter Adler

Peter Adler

foreword by
Marvin B. Scott

MOMENTUM

A Theory of Social Action

SAGE PUBLICATIONS Beverly Hills London

For information address:

SAGE Publications, Inc.
275 South Beverly Drive
Beverly Hills, California 90212

SAGE Publications Ltd
28 Banner Street
London EC1Y 8QE, England

Printed in the United States of America

Library of Congress Cataloging in Publication Data

Adler, Peter, 1951-
Momentum, a theory of social action.

(Sociological observations; 11)
Bibliography: p.
1. Collective behavior. 2. Social action. I. Title. II. Series.
HM299.A34 302 81-2718
ISBN 0-8039-1307-9 AACR2
ISBN 0-8039-1581-0 (pbk.)

FIRST PRINTING

TO PATTI

Ten years ago I had a dream.
Thanks for making it reality.

Contents

Foreword

In his play-by-play rendition of the struggles between the contending teams of Trojans and Greeks, Homer was the first sociologist to take as a topic of analysis the phenomenon of momentum—the forces that move people to extraordinary action.

But where Homer sings about the power within individuals that enables them to transcend themselves in acts of supreme accomplishment they possess the excellence of *arete*, Peter Adler, in the same sense, will talk about "second wind." And where Homer sings about the behind-the-scenes maneuvers of Zeus and Hera to explain the continual shift in momentum between Trojans and Greeks, Adler will suggest that collective emotion can be engineered in two directions—it can surge forward or fall back, depending on the tactical management of the situation. Same subject, different lingo.

Because the gods in Homer behave with patterned regularity, one can formulate precise laws that control their interference in human affairs. Momentum is the moment when gods interfere in human affairs, and thus Adler's book might be regarded as a study of the elementary forms of religious life.

Employing the Simmel-Goffmanesque method of systematic illustration, Adler pursues the notion that all of life has a dimension of momentum, of which the most readily identifiable forms in sports and speculation are but paradigm cases. The only precondition for the emergence of momentum is what

Goffman has called "action"—risky, problematic, and fateful situations voluntarily engaged in. It is, as Goffman noted, in occasions and places of action—casinos, pool halls, and racetracks—that we find our true places of worship. God is not present in the prayer before the Super Bowl, but in the ritualistic symbolism of the game. Inside the football stadium meticulous order prevails. The playing field is clearly marked, the scoreboard placed for all to see. The game demands absolute and supreme orderliness. At the smallest infraction of the rules, the umpire's whistle stops the game. In this ritualistically ordered world, Adler finds what he calls the "magic moment," "the charismatic play," and the "immortalizing achievement." In this world Achilles slays Hector, the Steelers destroy the Cowboys.

Besides sports, we find momentum operating (as Adler shows in great detail) in the stock market, the creative act, and intimate relations. In each of these settings, the players can be taken outside of themselves, literally in a state of ecstasy. Moments of momentum are moments of magic.

In sum, Adler's book is a highly original work that has the potential of leading to a rethinking of *the magical moments that make the world coherent.* If the implications of this are thought through, the study of social structure may bloom again with its original freshness, and the world will be seen as "the home of men who live with gods." By centering analysis on momentum, the sociological act of demystification will have the paradoxical effect of restoring a sense of enchantment. Adler is our guide into this wondrous world.

—Marvin B. Scott
Hunter College
City University of
New York

Acknowledgments

Completing books, like the specific arenas described herein, is very much a study in the establishment of momentum. As such, this endeavor has been helped greatly by the impetus given me through interaction with many key individuals. Without their help, this final product would never have come to fruition.

First, I want to thank the people closest to me, who encouraged me to attempt this "different" kind of work. Jack Douglas remained behind me throughout to make sure I never let down and quit. The great profundity of his own life's work will continue to be an inspiration to me. Fred Davis provided unerring support, steady counsel, and many constructive criticisms at all points along the way. Cesar Grana helped me to see the sacredness of everyday life, and especially in sports, directing my efforts toward looking at momentum as a "magical" force in the social world. In addition, Bennett Berger provided some much-needed focus, clarity, and professionalism to a roughly drafted first manuscript. John Johnson was not only enthusiastic about my pursuit of this topic from the beginning, but offered criticism, guidance and positive reinforcement throughout the endeavor. Finally, without the encouragement of Peter Manning the work simply would never have been completed.

Other close colleagues throughout my career in sociology buoyed my sometimes dying faith in the discipline and academia. Friends such as Dave Altheide, Marvin Cummins,

Murray Davis, Andy Fontana, Paul Rasmussen and Marvin Scott, through their own individual genius and creativity, convinced me to continue with this and other projects and to appreciate the pleasures of research and collegial communication.

Many other people showed interest in this work, providing friendship, helpful comments on critical portions of earlier drafts, and/or leads to important concepts and sources: Carl Bailey, David Briggs, John Gundersen, Rudolf Haerle, Joe Kotarba, Paul Lowenberg, Jim Morgan and Jim White. I am also grateful to Doris Osborne and Kay Giacomo for typing versions of the manuscript with the utmost quality and care.

My parents and in-laws showed pride, patience, belief, understanding and gave me the freedom to do what *I* thought was best. I hope that I shall continue to reflect their love and devotion.

My daughter, Jori, helped me maintain my sanity through otherwise trying times with her humorous diversions, and by giving me a sense of perspective in a sometimes absurd and chaotic world. Finally, words cannot sum up my gratitude, love and affection for my wife, Patti, to whom this book is dedicated. She had as much to say about the final product and was as deeply ingrained in all facets of the research as any other person could possibly be. I can never repay her for all she has done.

Nevertheless, any deletions, misinterpretations, deficiencies or errors found in the manuscript are totally my responsibility. But for any creativity, insights, accolades or illuminations, I share the rewards equally with the coterie of friends and colleagues who helped along the way. Thank you all.

—P.A.

1

INTRODUCTION

The term *momentum* describes a type of movement that is noticeable as unique among the many ordinary types of motion. Occurrences that capture this rare quality flow with an accelerated rhythm and intensity, whether they carry their participants soaring exuberantly onward or plunging despairingly backward. Yet, although momentum holds great significance as an elevated dynamic form and is a commonly shared social construction, the field of sociology has neglected to address it specifically as a human behavioral process.

To define momentum, let us first look at the writings of natural scientists, for the term has its roots in ancient physics. I shall refer to natural-science conceptions of momentum throughout this work in an attempt to lay some historical and interdisciplinary bases of understanding. They should be viewed, however, as metaphorical illustrations, sometimes contrasting, sometimes analogous with the present study, for I seek to clarify the momentum of people, not objects. Early philosophers of matter conceived of momentum as a quality of movement involving an object's speed, acceleration, and power.

Modern physicists have refined this into a calculable force arising through a combination of mass and velocity.

In individual and group social life, momentum also involves the velocity or change of velocity with which actions are accomplished. A collective's or idea's momentum is the dynamic intensity that propels it through the layers of social resistance toward some desired or feared destiny. However, speed is not the only element that characterizes the complexity of this force. In fact, momentum describes the entire process through which action occurs, encompassing rate, grace, intensity, effort, and success.

This work is a conceptual study, examining the way momentum is perceived, interpreted, and acted upon in everyday life. I have selected momentum as a topic because it is a basic "folk" idea, used by many to refer to an elite type of action. My aim is to provide all those interested in studying the intricacies of human behavior with a new analytical tool, one which describes a recurrent pattern of individual and group action in a scientifically clear and precise manner. In addition, I hope to draw attention away from the static and structural side of human behavior by focusing on a dynamic facet of life. All existence has an ebb and flow, yet this often goes unrecognized by those who formulate "blueprint" models of life or incorporate a model of the "composite" or "average" actor. In fact, there is nothing average about the social force carried by momentum; it is the charged flow of people acting at their peaks or nadirs. We either coast easily through difficult obstacles or become mired in the simplest tasks, sinking deeper into ineptitude. Momentum theory is thus offered as a short-term alternative to another "folk" concept: the law of averages. Human behavior, I assert, does not occur in a totally random manner, with success and failure evening themselves out to produce regular mediocrity. Rather, behavior often follows a momentum model where success and failure occur by turns. Thus, a person who has built up motivation and morale, started an activity, and received early positive feedback, would be expected to continue producing good work (assuming the temporary absence of momentum breakers). Conversely, someone who has repeatedly experienced frustration, psychological blockage, and an inability to accomplish something will not be expected suddenly to blossom into great creative success. Beyond life's ordinary vicissitudes, streaks and slumps occur, and this is where momentum becomes important. I offer a description and analysis of the internal workings of this behavioral process, from the conditions preceding its occurrence to those inciting, feeding, and sustaining it, and finally to those puncturing it.

THE SOCIAL CONSTRUCTION OF MOMENTUM

In so doing, my focus will be on the perspectives held by involved participants—on their beliefs concerning the absence or presence and rise and fall of momentum—for no matter how concrete or objective an item's existence in the social world may seem, it is inevitably colored by the human beings perceiving, interpreting, and using it. This is especially true for something as ephemeral and intangible as momentum, for it describes a social process that can easily be misconstructed or wished into being and is highly shaped by the context framing its occurrence.

People, with their subjective capacities for observing and assessing what they encounter, react in varied ways to others who possess momentum. Momentum may thus be sensed during its absence or overlooked during its presence. What becomes significant to the interaction process, then, is not whether momentum occurs but whether or not it is perceived to exist. In sport, for example, an athlete may react with despondency to the perception of his or her opponent's momentum, while another, not noticing anything, suffers no setback at all. Here we see how the truth value of momentum's occurrence becomes secondary to the meaning value ascribed to it by participants, conceptions of all "exterior reality" being subjugated by human actors' feelings and thoughts.

Such subjective perception becomes the basis upon which shared attitudes and beliefs are formed. Hence, like all joint understandings and actions, momentum must be recognized as a *constructed* and *negotiated* aspect of social life. In a political race, for example, it is the consensus formed by the amorphous "press" that usually influences the public's perception of a candidate's momentum and may then affect mass sentiment about him or her.

People's manners of communicating with others can greatly affect the formation of group interpretations of and reactions to momentum's presence. As Goffman has shown us, individual and collective self-presentation is a key factor in concealing, revealing, or disguising the degree of momentum at hand. Such impressions fall into two categories: intentional and unintentional. Most of the time people do not consciously plan an impression strategy that communicates their inner intensity and amount of generated thrust. If they consider this variable at all, they will let others view their motivation just as it is. But there are a number of circumstances where people consciously try to transmit a social message about their momentum potential for the purpose of influencing both themselves and others. Whether their intent is to stimulate, intimidate, impress, or evoke sympathy, interaction can be managed to convey both the type and the degree of momentum possessed.

Shared symbolic meanings can at any time become attached to particular actions, associating them with momentum or stigmatizing them as unable to produce it. When the social perception of momentum's presence becomes aroused (as in a craps game where one player is seen as "hot"), the excitement quickly spreads, drawing others into the rising fervor and blending strangers into a group that cheers and shouts as one. Once this streak has been assessed as completed, social boundaries are once again reasserted and individual lines of interest reemerge. Such circumstances provide a fertile background for the "placebo effect," such as Frank (1961) documents in the medical sphere, which can create the acknowledgment of momentum and lead to its social consequences without the presence of any genuine, initial boost. What usually follows is the actual generation of momentum from this spurious base. This placebo effect can also operate in reverse, clamping down on aroused intensity and convincing people that momentum has vanished. This process is related to the "self-fulfilling" and "suicidal" (self-negating) prophesies Merton (1968) discusses, where group interpretations of the present and future tend to become reality precisely because they are given mass credence and acted upon as fact.

My approach to the study of momentum thus draws on contemporary existential (Douglas and Johnson, 1977) and absurdist (Lyman and Scott, 1970) sociology and their sociological and philosophical predecessors: symbolic interactionism, dramaturgical sociology, phenomenology, existentialist philosophy, and pragmatism. These perspectives view human actors as dynamic thinking and feeling beings who continuously make sense out of an intrinsically meaningless reality. Through their own subjective and sometimes shared perceptions and interpretations of what they encounter, they forge a series of evolving definitions of situations, and act on the basis of the beliefs that they form. Their activities represent a conscious selection from among several alternatives they have envisioned and weighed. This conscious intentionality, with related emotions and motivations feeding into it and behavioral acts emerging from it, serves as the basic impetus for individual and collective interactional momentum, the focus of my study.

HISTORY OF MOMENTUM

The concept of momentum can trace its roots to earliest recorded history, to the great intellectual foundations of the Hellenic period. But this heritage applies only to natural-science concerns with momentum; never before has there been a social scientific inquiry into momentum per se. Early civilizations laid the groundwork for more sophisticated momentum studies by focusing on the movement of earthly and celestial objects to discover universal laws governing interplanetary mobility. Their concerns have been adopted and expanded by their scientific descendants, who eventually incorporated such interests as motion, the derivatives of motion (impetus, velocity, acceleration), types of motion, and the results of motion. Let us briefly review the history of scientific thought related to momentum.

The Ancient Thinkers

One of the basic questions posed by the Greeks concerned the ultimate source of motion. Physical-science philosophers of the pre-Socratic era believed that nature carried within itself a quasi-living source of movement. Aristole (384-322 B.C.) was in accord with this assumption and postulated that elements move in the direction of their "natural" place in the universe (upwards for fire and air, downwards for earth and water) with a speed directly proportional to their weight. Once they arrive, they resume their natural state of rest.

Preserved into the Middle Ages by the Arab civilization, Aristotle's philosophy was adopted with zeal by the religious scholars of the Church. Aquinas and other moral philosophers of that era held to a dogmatic view of what they now termed "scholasticism," proclaiming that the order and motion of the universe reflected God's perfect acts of creation. The divine source summoned objects and inspired them to seek their natural positions. It was in this climate that Galileo arose to propose his new ideas.

The Creation of Classical Mechanics

Oft denounced as a heretic because of his refutation of Aristotle's beliefs, Galileo (1564-1642) tried to disprove two of his predecessor's main contentions. One famous tale suggests that he dropped two objects of unequal weight from the Leaning Tower of Pisa to demonstrate that their speed was similar, and not proportional to their weight. He also denied that falling bodies achieve top speed instantaneously, suggesting instead a continuous build-up of acceleration. The implications of his reformulations concerning the onset of movement are germane to momentum theory. Social examples of both Aristotle's earlier view and Galileo's later one can be found in the way human beings begin an activity. At times we see the instantaneous jump to rapid velocity that Aristotle imagined, particularly in the "spark start" so characteristic of explosive momentum. But the gradual increase of velocity postulated by

Galileo is also frequently evident, especially for cases of placid momentum.

Another of Galileo's contributions was the abstract idea of a vacuum, with corresponding theoretical laws about how objects would behave under such a condition. This eliminated the need for calculating the resistance effect of air and other matter. However, Galileo may be best known for proposing the ultimate resistance tendency, the *principle of inertia*: "a body moving on a level surface will continue in the same direction at constant speed unless disturbed" (March, 1970: 23). Objects, whether moving or at rest, he felt, will continue in a constant pattern, tenaciously withstanding any change in their velocity until resistant forces intercede. Extrapolating to momentum, this suggests that both movement and its absence will ideally persist until challenged rather than simply start up or slow down as a result of timing.

Closely following Galileo's advances, Leibniz (1646-1716) sought to explicate "natural inertia" by examining the difficulties involved in moving stationary objects. He proposed the idea of reciprocal *action* and *reaction*, wherein acting forces are in turn equally reacted upon by others (see Weiner, 1951: 101-102). The notion of active and passive forces further intrigued him, and he ultimately refined the former into two segments: *primitive force*, representing the primary active agent, and *derivative force*, arising out of the efforts and results of the initial impetus (see Gabbey, 1971: 5). As we will see, these two types of force can be recognized in a variety of social actions and institutions.

The next major contributor to the scientific revolution unleashed by Galileo was Descartes (1596-1650). This French philosopher focused on the nature and properties of collisions between objects. What are the effects, he asked, on both the body in motion and the one at rest when the two meet? The same question can be asked today for all types of opposing elements (as in sport) both possessing and lacking momentum. In order to solve this puzzle, Descartes propounded the law of *conservation of momentum*: "When two bodies collide, the sum of their momenta will not change" (March, 1970: 29). Momentum, to him, was "quantity of motion," or the force created by multiplying a moving body's weight and velocity. Thus, in a collision, force could be transferred or rearranged but not lost. Not only is momentum conserved in a simple two-party collision, but a constant amount of force is conserved throughout the universe.

In his study of collisions, Descartes described several possible outcomes of two-party encounters. When a heavier or more rapidly moving body encounters one with lesser force, the latter will yield and be moved by the former. Further, the body with greater initial momentum will expend some of its force in overcoming the resistance of the other, which absorbs the energy and makes it its own. This exemplifies the *contest view of force*: Bodies of unequal momentum vie for domination, the stronger emerging as victorious.

Sometimes objects fail to follow this adhesive pattern, but react instead with *elasticity*. In this case they rebound from each other while conserving the total original momentum. Here, one party is forced backward with a *negative momentum*, while the other advances forward with an added positive thrust. Occasionally we even see *explosive* collisions where objects ignite each other and burst apart in opposing directions. The total momentum is still conserved as the extreme negative force of one counterbalances the positive strength of the other.

Descartes finally considers the situation of *zero momentum*. This occurs when the center of mass, or balance point, does not move. Two forces of equal momentum (i.e., a lighter object moving twice as fast as its doubly heavy counterpart) can meet, or touch and pass, so that they cancel each other out and their effect on the outside environment is nil.

The greatest achievement of this period belongs to Newton (1642-1727), who took the questions, inspirations, and advances of his predecessors and combined them with his own insights into a complete theory of mechanics. Newton's main concern was with understanding how objects overcame inertia to achieve momentum, which he believed could result only through the interaction of objects with each other (and their reciprocal influence). He began by reviewing and clarifying his definition of terms. *Velocity* was the rate of change of position, or the state of motion. *Acceleration* (Galileo) was the rate of change of velocity. *Force* referred to the strength of the body responsible for the change. *Impulse* was a locomotive power or quality which moves, but only through a finite distance in a given time (Gabbey, 1971). *Mass*, his own creation, indicated an object's capacity to resist motion, drawing on both its density and bulk. *Momentum* was thus the product of mass and velocity. His famous laws of motion are as follows:

Law I.	Every body continues in its state of rest or of uniform motion unless compelled to change by another force.
Law II.	The rate of change of momentum is proportional to the force pressing upon it.
Law III.	To every action there is always an equal and opposing reaction.

In the first law we recognize a restatement of Galileo's principle of inertia. The second law specifies a direct relation between bodies and components of the universe (in effect, force equals the product of mass and acceleration). This was instrumental in Newton's illumination of the laws of gravity. When he discovered the constant force exerted by gravity he was able to resolve the Aristotle/Galileo impasse concerning the speed of falling bodies. Newton learned that a falling object reaches a *terminal velocity* where acceleration ceases because the air resistance to the fall comes to equal the force propelling the object downward.

It is the third law, however, that carried the greatest implications for the new science of mechanics. As Leibniz had begun to understand, all actions and reactions are inseparable. To Newton this meant that the active and passive forces are really part of one interaction and hence always equal. This refutes the traditional contest approach to force and inspires the

Newtonian one: Bodies only offer as much resistance as is necessary to overcome the push they receive. Thus, the image is of equal rather than unequal forces exerting pressure on each other, with the remaining energy flowing over to give momentum to the grouping.

SOCIOLOGY AND MOMENTUM

Although there are several areas of sociology to which momentum theory would be relevant, the discipline contains little in its scholarly offerings that directly addresses this topic. The greatest relevance lies in the theories on collective behavior, where the structure and dynamics assemblages varying in sizes, from small groups to mass publics, are discerned. I will begin by addressing Blumer's conception of social organizations, outline the views of the imitation/contagion school, and then discuss Smelser's ideas on the forging of collective beliefs and actions.

Social Organization

Blumer (1951) distinguishes among four different types of elementary collective groupings: the acting crowd, the expressive crowd, the mass, and the public. Acting crowds (i.e., angry mobs) are composed of groups of people in close contact who are purposefully directed toward a goal or objective. Expressive crowds, while physically united, plan to accomplish no specific activity and focus on the build-up and release of emotions (i.e., dancing at religious revivals). Both forms of crowds display the contagion process characterized by "interpersonal milling," "interstimulation," and "circular reaction" (to be discussed more fully below). Masses are psychologically unified by a common concern, but lack the physical propinquity often associated with generating high excitement and intensity. Their communication must often be from a distance, yet they maintain alignment of action (i.e., political movements). Publics constitute the most dispersed and least affiliated groups, having neither personal contact nor shared interests (i.e., television audiences). Their membership in the group usually depends on receiving the mass media's one-way communication. Those groups that are most structurally and organizationally predisposed toward developing momentum are acting crowds and masses, with their goal-oriented focus and diverse, yet still functioning, means of communication.

Imitation and Contagion

This area encompasses a concern with how emotional excitement becomes intensified as it spreads among people in physically united groups. Here, snowballing imitation and contagion can be seen to develop inner momentum through their expansion processes: the *momentum of contagion.* This literature also addresses the unification of separate individuals into a cohesive group, an element crucial to developing the social integration necessary to collective momentum (as in team units). Here we see the collective groundwork for *contagion of momentum*, the way momentum is communicated and diffused through the processes of imitation and contagion. Third, the transmission of feelings and ideas, part of the momentum diffusion process, is examined, and different models incorporating varying degrees of explanatory value are offered. We will begin by surveying the seminal contributions of Tarde and Le Bon, and follow with their thematic descendants.

Tarde, writing at the turn of the nineteenth century, is best known for his social psychological work on imitation and suggestion. In *The Laws of Imitation* (1890), he refers to this repetitive (imitative) process as a primary means for the "transmission, constancy and spread of social forms." Imitation functions initially in a socializing role, facilitating the intergenerational transference of social meanings and cultural norms. Operating among contemporaries too, it passes customs, fashions, and the use of new inventions outward from a central point. Tarde saw imitation as a consciously rational act, especially where social inferiors aspire to resemble their superiors. Positing a model for this development, he described the growth of "wants" as characterized by a slow start followed by rapid acceleration and then gradual leveling.

His interest then transferred to crowds and the public in a work on opinion and the mob (1901). "Crowds" were defined as groups of people who, when united in time and space, join together through a series of emotions, beliefs, and actions. "Publics," in contrast, may share common attitudes and ideas but they lack a unifying bond. Tarde's contributions were influential for both contemporaries and later generations.

One such compatriot and peer, Le Bon, was inspired by Durkheim as well as Tarde. His 1897 study, *The Crowd*, endeavors to examine the process of contagion in crowd behavior. Psychologically organized masses (as distinct from mere assemblages of people) are subject to the "law of the mental unity of crowds." This total unification requires the complete disappearance of conscious individual personalities. In their place a "collective mind" is forged out of the combined unconscious characteristics of the group. Le Bon emphasized the crude nature of this new entity, attributing this to instinctual, racial, and evolutionary factors carried genetically. Stripped of the conscious veneer of civilized rationality, the group spirit loses the higher, more intelligent features of humanity. What remains are the primitive, ignoble traits of earlier savage times. Thus, crowds are not really capable of intelligent behavior, although they can act heroically as well as destructively.[1]

Le Bon also highlights three situational factors affecting the popular mind's formation. The sentiment of "invincible power," gained from the sheer mass of people, causes individuals to yield to instincts they would otherwise be able to control. Second, the process of "contagion" hypnotizes people, making them sacrifice their personal interests for the group. Most significant, "suggestibility" develops, rendering individuals highly receptive to the recommendations of others and no longer guided by their own will.

Le Bon's depiction of the Durkheimian collective mind emphasizes the emotional, irrational, and irresponsible aspects of crowd behavior generated by the loss of individual consciousness. The mystical, hypnotic images of contagion and suggestibility constitute equally nonreasoned explanations of how feelings and acts spread. A clear contrast can thus be drawn, separating this from Tarde's rational, intentional view of imitation.

In the 1920s, however, a new perspective arose, synthesizing the two earlier approaches. Sociologists of the Chicago school (see Ross, 1905; Park and Burgess, 1921; Park, 1972) adopted an interest in crowds, publics, group behavior, and other topics Tarde and Le Bon had pursued. But this cohort was of a more empirical bent, disdaining the mysticism Le Bon had ascribed to the collective spirit. Instead, they placed explanatory value in human interaction. The interpersonal effects of crowd activity were seen to emanate from close physical proximity, the hypnotic excitement of mass arousal, and general milling behavior. Thus, the Chicago school retained Le Bon's depiction of crowds as emotional, unpredictable, and suggestible, but augmented this with Tarde's belief in the purposeful and reflective nature of imitation. The orientation forged by the Chicago school remains largely unchanged to this date.

Two contemporary sociologists provide us with diverse examples of the current imitation/contagion school. Blumer (1951), long fascinated by collective behavior, proposed a model for the "circular reaction" process he had observed in crowds. As people become emotionally aroused, he notes, they infect their neighbors with feelings of excitement. These stimuli get absorbed, reflected, and retransmitted to both the original senders and others. An "interstimulation" thus develops, wherein individuals reflect each other's states of feeling, thereby heightening them (echoing Newton's theory of reciprocal influence). Blumer underscores the aroused, erratic, and suggestible nature of these moments, which differentiates them from usual interpretative behavior.

Couch (1970), however, envisions this process as occurring within a quasi-normal interpretative framework. He argues that because people in crowds continue to engage in role-taking, they maintain social and symbolic sensitivity. In taking the role of the neighboring other, people react by projecting the other's outward appearance upon their inner selves. This facilitates their aligning their actions together identically. Couch posits an essentially imitative view of behavior that rests on mass "visual monitoring" to keep individuals abreast of new developments. Thus, his analysis of crowd interaction stresses cognitive assessments over emotional immersion. Yet Couch still maintains that this behavior is nonrational, because the rapidity of parallel responsiveness leaves insufficient time to think adequately before acting.

In sum, we are presented with a continuum of interpretations describing the causes and nature of social contagion from the extremely rationalistic to the hysterically emotional. Nearly the full range of these can serve as possible explanations for momentum diffusion within the group, depending on particular circumstances. In the Le Bonian and Blumerian analyses, the feelings and emotions transmitted through various means are actually manifestations of a momentum that has gripped the crowd. This represents the explosive, aroused form of momentum that is most common. But the more placid, reasoned type and spread can also occur, as Tarde and Couch document, where frenzy is replaced by relaxation and activation is primarily mental. Thus, depending on the setting (i.e., the emotional display of a political revolt versus the stock market's relative restraint) and the individuals involved (i.e., sports fans versus poker players), all of these imitation/contagion models (with one exception[2]) can serve as viable depictions of how momentum is generated, augmented, and circularly returned to cause restimulation on an interpersonal, social level.

Collective Beliefs and Actions

Smelser (1962) proposes a theory of collective behavior designed to explain how people become unified and propelled into intense forms of collective action (panics, crazes, hostile outbursts, and the like). He defines collective action as "mobilization on the basis of a belief which redefines social action." For us, here, the centrally important characteristic is the belief: those factors leading up to it, and the way it reshapes the definition of the situation (and hence human group activity). Smelser posits a "value-added" progression, where each development is seen as part of a fixed logical sequence that leads toward the increasingly certain collective outcome. In order for a situation to build into one of these intense behavioral movements there must be structural conduciveness within the setting (ruthlessness, volatility, fluidity), structural strain (ambiguity, uncertainty, lack of control, unpredictability), the growth and spread of a generalized belief (that things are about to radically worsen or improve), precipitating factors (a dramatic illustration confirming the belief), mobilization of the participants for action (due to the development of concrete fear or certain optimism), and the presence throughout of social control mechanisms (be they legal, normative, or individual).

Smelser's typology forms a conceptual frame into which the development of collective momentum readily fits. The factors he describes can easily be seen to generate many of momentum's necessary components, from behavioral goals through motivation, emotion, arousal, and action. His ideas complement many of my own and can be used throughout to further our understanding of the structural and interactional processes facilitating momentum.

The remainder of this work presents the theory I propose and the empirical descriptions of its occurrence. In Chapter 2, I present my general theory of momentum, beginning with a definition of momentum's basic components, forms and sequences. I discuss momentum as a social force, comparing it with the momentum of objects, examining the effects of various environmental influences on its character, considering the relationship between force and momentum, indicating various reservoirs of power and their effects, and showing how momentum affects the self, both as a whole and in parts. I close the chapter with a detailed schematic model of momentum that illustrates the evolution of momentum's rise, sustenance, and conclusion, incorporating all the components and forces and showing their contribution to the complete spiraling process.

Chapters 3-5 present my examination of three settings, chosen because of their overlaps and contrasts. Here I try to show how momentum is affected by structural and situational constraints, varying in appearance with people and surroundings. These thus provide an opportunity to see momentum transformed from an abstract definition into a series of concretely lodged examples. I consider the world of sport first, where athletes vie for the excellence and domination momentum can bring on physical, psychological, and social levels. Both individual and team orientations are crucial here, enabling us to witness the dynamics of momentum within the solitary person and small groups. Chapter 4 examines the stock market, where the complex interweavings of multifarious self-directed and jointly grouped individuals form mass action. Macropolitical, macrosocial, and macroeconomic events and trends indirectly color momentum here, as they are perceived and interpreted by the flurried activities of participants trading on the basis of multiple aims, patterns, and perspectives. I then shift from focusing on one particular scene at a time to a conglomeration of generalized social behavior in my discussion of momentum in everyday life. In Chapter 5 I consider the actions of abstract individuals and how the performance of certain activities is affected by and in return affects momentum. Background investigation into human rhythmicity sets the stage, after which momentum is considered as it relates to task achievement, affective relationships, the broad span of careers, and finally collective behavior. In concluding each of these chapters I assess their relation to the other settings and to the general portrayal of momentum. The final chapter summarizes the contributions and implications of this study and the benefits that can be obtained from using momentum as an analytical tool.

NOTES

1. It is interesting to compare Le Bon's view of crowd psychology with Freud's definition. Although there are many similarities, Freud (writing in direct rebuttal to Le Bon) maintained that no such thing as the group mind ever formed, and that the characteristics unique to crowd behavior are caused by the bonds uniting these otherwise unconnected individuals. Freud also believed that within crowds people always maintain their separate identities, although they were easily provoked to collective thought and action by the mass hypnotic effect.

2. Of all the theories, the sole component I would designate as unsuitable for transference to a description of momentum expansion is Le Bon's image of the group mind. Even in the utmost heat of passion, where spirit and arousal are high, there is never such a complete loss of ego as to submerge totally the consciousness of individuality, or lose inner will and guidance entirely. In fact, people often use this aspect of the group-mind theory as an excuse for irrational behavior.

2

TOWARD A GENERAL THEORY OF MOMENTUM

Momentum's existence, although documented by scientists in the physical world, remains an elusive, and to this point undefined, element of the social world. Not a mystical or purely sensate phenomenon, it is born, bred, and maintained during the normal course of human existence. As such, its occurrence can be described, dissected, and explained. It is the goal of this chapter to do just that.

DEFINING MOMENTUM

In Chapter 1, I described momentum as a state of dynamic intensity marked by an elevated or depressed rate of motion, grace, and success. These are but superficial impressions of its effects; they describe the product of momentum but not how it functions or comes to be internally created. Let us look at some defining features that are universal to its existence and some diverse forms it can assume.

Components of Momentum

It is often difficult to distinguish between momentum, inertia, and the various intermediary forms of more common movement. Inertia can be recognized by a listless passivity in which effort is either totally absent or is unable to produce a course of action. Here the individual or collective either drifts aimlessly with the social tide or rests immobile.

Momentum, in contrast, results from a purposeful striving for accomplishment. Attention becomes centrally focused on a specific *goal* or end state, ranging in nature from the short-term or frivolous to the long-term crux of identity and existence. Whether this goal evolves over a lengthy planning period or arises spontaneously, it creates an awareness of relative distance between the present state and the ideal, highlighting the measurement of progress toward and regression away from the goal. This selection of an aim thus inspires a point toward which effort and output can ultimately be directed and behavior concentrated. A secondary function of the goal is to demarcate the boundaries of momentum's occurrence: It does not ordinarily begin prior to intentional striving or last much beyond the objective's attainment. Thus, momentum is not ignited by aimless, wandering behavior (although the early stages of involvement with an activity, before focusing occurs, may resemble this). For any enterprise to rise above the ordinary it must be purposely directed along a conscious path toward a specific end; only this concentration can inspire the fullness of performance and intensity which characterizes momentum.

Intimately interconnected with the perception and internalization of a goal is the *motivation* launching the effort to conquer it. Historically, two competing schools of thought exist concerning motivation. *Drive theories* focus on the instincts (James, 1890; McDougall, 1910, 1923), inner tensions (Lewin, 1935), needs (Maslow, 1943), and/or irrational inner forces (Freud, 1922, 1948) that propel people toward a goal. *Incentive theories*, such as Plato's traditional rationalism, emphasize free will and the human conscious ability to evaluate and select rationally from among the goals society offers. During this process of choosing a goal and evoking the motivation to achieve it, I see both internal and external motivational pulls and pressures as continually asserting themselves. Human beings then assess and select a goal according to its relative urgency and shifting situational factors. Thus, a vibrant will and desire to attain the chosen goal arises, which inspires the decisions to seek an end and continuously organizes, directs, and channels efforts toward its fulfillment. Without this coordination and thrust, the envisioned path would remain unapproached and potential energy sources untapped and unharnessed. Momentum, then, is dependent on the presence of intentional motivation, whether this arises prior to the onset of action or sometimes during its course.

Emotional feelings then become highly entwined with the focusing on a goal and the urgency of the motivational drive to attain it. Reactions are evoked to the poignancy of the individual or group condition which the lack of that goal breeds, and to the sensation of what its achievement would signify. Violent frustration, hate, anger, pride, and elation exemplify the zeal of immediate emotions experienced, making momentum a condition of heightened dramatic quality (as differentiated from the calm rationality of mundane existence). Like motivation, there are conflicting views about the nature and role of emotion vis-à-vis human action. One point of contention, for example, revolves around whether emotions promote disorganization or directedness. Those schools that view emotion as a dizzying array of sentimentality, including the arousal theorists, claim it disrupts clarity and is therefore detrimental to positive momentum. Others, feeling that emotion gives form to heightened feelings, view it in an augmenting role. In either case, once motion toward the goal gets under way, the sense of making clear progress yields a feeling of power and ability that is inherently pleasurable. People recognize that they are acting closer to peak potential and achieve inner satisfaction—what Maslow (1943) calls self-actualization. The long-term emotional result of positive momentum is a strongly ingrained sense of confidence that can boost a personal or collective sense of self-esteem, approach to a problem, and future ability to achieve momentum.

Another recognizably symptomatic feature of the momentum process is *arousal*. When a person becomes excited, bodily reaction occurs first in the conscious mind (activation). Initial impact (effect) of the momentum-precipitating factor, then, is to elevate the activation level. The mind then triggers a series of responses throughout the body, which, in turn, experiences a more general arousal. This build-up and release of energy is not associated with channeling into a particular direction; rather, it is nonspecific. As people become aroused, available resources of physiological, cognitive, and interpersonal energy are called forth to heightened levels of intensification. Sensitivity and speed of reaction are then raised by increased activity among sensory nerve receptors that become attuned to the flow of excitement and adrenaline (see Malmo, 1959; Bindra, 1968; Hebb, 1955). Inner reflectiveness and communicative networks are also brought to peak capacity, thus evoking a maximum degree of preparedness. Whether outwardly displayed or inwardly controlled, this arousal serves as a potent springboard to action.

Perhaps the most recognizable aspect of momentum is the *elevated performance* it yields, raising the quality and/or quantity of achievement to a plane often "over the heads" of those possessing it. Pace and tempo transformations then occur, either accelerating movement to a feverish rate or slowing it to an unhurried, deliberate grace (varying with the positive and negative forms I shall discuss below). A marked *rhythmicity* is thus instituted, giving momentum a smooth, synchronized character, unlike the often erratic and percussive cadence of routine, everyday life. The regular symmetry of this cyclical pulsation promotes a continuing acceleration of force, because the ongoing harmonious beat prevents accumulated power from dissipating and guides the individual or group along an escalating track.

While several of the preceding characteristics are occasionally found in forms of movement lacking momentum, the following remaining features are almost exclusively momentum-related. Here, we note the universal presence of an internally self-generating mechanism in operation. With individuals, groups, and social institutions alike, a *circular feedback system* develops through which accomplishments already achieved are instrumental in aiding further propulsion. As people developing momentum react to the sense of satisfaction (or frustration) generated by coworkers and responsive outside others, a recycled source of impetus is made available to fuel further motion. Energy already spent can thus be partially recaptured and coupled with the continuing output of fresh effort, making subsequent progress toward the goal easier. As each new wave of productive energy becomes converted into tangible achievement and then tapped to be fed back for reuse, another *spiral* of the burgeoning momentum process is forged. A dynamic, internally circular process is thus envisioned, whereby input and output are continually reutilized to maintain a high level of velocity. *"Coasting"* (key to momentum) demonstrates the existence of this inner propulsion phenomenon, for when new energy ceases to be fed into the system, movement does not halt abruptly; instead it carries on in a gradually diminishing fashion, powered temporarily by the impulse extracted from the recycled feedback. This cycle can continue indefinitely until broken by some outside force, crippled by internal weakening, or voluntarily relinquished.

Interrelation of Components

None of these factors is singly capable of creating momentum without the full presence of all the others. Rather, they are symbiotically interconnected, so that once more than one element falls into place, they tend to induce the full complement's rise. When all together, they function synergistically, reinforcing and promoting each other's presence to blend as one in the total process. Thus, only through a *synchronization of subsystems*, with all vital ingredients interlocked and feeding into the spiraling model, can momentum be achieved. Although it is complex and often difficult to achieve, this seems to be a behavioral pattern that arises naturally in human beings and the social institutions they power.

Within this overarching description of momentum's characteristics and function there is still room for considerable variation. Several distinct forms emerge that represent typical patterns of momentum's occurrence.

Toward one extreme we have *explosive* momentum, a fast-moving, excitable state that is less marked by synchrony than intensity. Often launched rapidly, a fragility surrounds this plateau that enables it to come crashing down just as impetuously as it arose. In these instances the empowered body moves with great vigor and strength, hurdling barriers with ease and flair. Momentum spirals upward into a state of frenzy, continuing in this highly charged condition until the energy is somehow broken and the spiral shatters or descends to a more mundane level and dissolves.

At the other end of the spectrum we find *placid* momentum, a performative state that displays a calm, unhurried grace. Often slipped into gradually and in a less noticeable fashion than its explosive counterpart, it enables its possessor to glide through obstacles with a settled but steady surety. Here, rapid tempo is less important than relaxed and rhythmic pacing. In fact, outward displays of arousal may diminish while they are being internally absorbed by the powerful serenity of this securely grooved process. Although this form is often slower to arise and more leisurely moving, it is buoyed by a quiet confidence and strong interrelation of component features that makes it more difficult to dislodge. Modifications of these two forms can be found, but they usually lean toward one or the other side of the continuum, rather than toward the center.

In addition to this differentiation, there are also the diametrically opposed *positive* and *negative* forms of momentum. These share a similar range of behavioral styles but move the individual or group in divergent directions. Positive momentum aids movement toward the goal while its negative counterpart moves the goal further from reach. In contrast, momentum's antithesis, inertia, precludes *any* change of position in relation to the goal (although the whole situation may drift with the background flow of evolution). Positive momentum is the most commonly appearing of these two modes, and use of the term without further modification refers to this form. Negative momentum develops less often, since it is rarely welcomed, and upon first being perceived is usually intentionally avoided. It generally results from thwarted efforts to attain the desired end, which have metamorphosed into an uncontrollable cycle of anxiety, depression, fear, and failure.

Ideally, these two forms should correspond as mirror images, but in practice they do not. Again and again we discern an urgent intensity, acceleration, and concentration that is more indigenous to the destructive, depressing force than to optimistic, uplifting action. The extremities of positive propulsion are thus restrained by caution and insecurity, while recurrent fear and self-doubt exacerbate the escalation of negative arousal and emotional reaction, plunging downfall and despair to more precipitous, overwhelming troughs.

Social Forces Affecting Momentum

In influencing the quality and rate of human beings' progress, momentum is itself subject to being influenced by social forces in the world. The first of these is the *resistance force* offered by society. Although social evolution is continuous, it does not occur without first overcoming the plethora of factors serving to deter any alteration in the status quo and to wear down the power of change. Social structure offers resistance to a gust of momentum sweeping in and changing the order through its institutionalized and often static blueprint for existence. Social attitudes and beliefs offer resistance to momentum by constituting a set of assumptions that must sometimes be put aside to achieve momentum, and/or that momentum occasionally threatens to cast into doubt. Even the ordinary ebb and flow of life serves to resist momentum by breaking any rhythmical, continuously mounting pattern with its erratic variations in pace and energy. The difficulty of coordinating individual or joint action is also a form of resistance pressure against momentum, since communication must function smoothly and effectively for a dynamic thrust to arise. Resistance force can thus be found in a plethora of obstacles, ranging from the grand to the petty and from the broadly abstract to the narrowly concrete, being lodged both within and outside of individuals and groups. Before any movement can commence, the resistance against it must first be combatted and the pressure to slow down fought throughout the entire sequence.

Set against this pressure are the two forces powering momentum. *Primitive force* (a social derivation of Leibniz's conception) is the fresh impulse that provides the initial drive. It is rooted in the innately dynamic character of human beings and their desire to achieve. Social conventions and expectations reinforce this boost by rewarding those who accomplish and denigrating those displaying little effort. Many social institutions also help to foster this primitive effort by providing a helping hand to those in difficulty (charities, for example) and encouraging others to surge ahead through incentive funds (grants, for example).

Derivative force arises as the effect of primitive force's early productivity is noticed by its creator and others. Those observing the results of that initial action form an evaluation of it that is perceived and absorbed by the creator through the circular feedback process. In reacting to the opinions held by both him or herself and others, the creator is spurred to additional energy and drive which can then be channeled into further creative acts. The earlier effort can thus be reutilized after it is partially recaptured and converted into reactive, or derivative, force. Not found in instances of solely impulsive outbursts, derivative force is thus a part of the self-generating phenomenon and fuels the carry-through process. Societal manifestations of derivative force include those projects or people insisting on a certain amount of achievement by the receiving party before they will provide secondary aid (i.e., matching funds contributions and investment tax credits).

These three forces all operate on a variety of levels, from the purely physiological to the psychological and social. We shall encounter their influences both aiding and hindering momentum in many concrete forms throughout the empirical settings that will be considered.

Sequential Model of Momentum

When momentum occurs it generally follows a path through certain stages from start to finish. I call this progression of rise and fall the "momentum sequence," and it can be observed in all the empirical arenas I shall examine.

Before any distinguishable momentum can occur, there must be a period devoted to *preparation*. During this phase the goals are set and the will to reach them becomes established. One or several plans of action may be considered and launched, but the true dynamic thrust remains as yet elusive; this can depend on an outside source or on the further development of internal readiness.

The first outwardly visible sign of momentum's onset is lodged in the *impetus* that powers the initial surge. Activation and energization occur, lifting activity onto a higher plane of functioning. Here the impulse is at last successful in creating a primary movement in the desired (or dreaded) direction. But the impulse which characterizes the initial creation of momentum is fleeting, lasting no more than a "knife-edge present"—one which appears but does not endure.

What is needed to initiate momentum fully is a drive that occupies a "specious present"—one with temporal duration and symbolic significance.[1] Here the spark of impetus catches hold, producing an ignition felt throughout the entire self, group, or movement. Only then is the primary thrust able to be recycled into re-generated force and the spiraling form created. This phase, constituting the *carry-through* of initial effort into the construction of a lasting propulsion (albeit still temporally bounded) is finally capable of effecting real progress toward the goal. The height of momentum obtained may vary from instance to instance, even fluctuating within a single occurrence, but the initial dynamics follow a similar progression.

Eventually all momentum comes to an end, however, and the period of *denouement* occurs. Conclusions can unfold suddenly or slowly, with momentum being cut off abruptly or winding down gradually. Thus, in some instances the degree of momentum will have declined to a low level by the point of termination, while in others termination leaves an extremely potent but static force remaining.

MOMENTUM AS A SOCIAL FORCE

Momentum, as observed throughout this work, involves the quality of movement toward a goal. As such, it encompasses the *process* people follow in pursuing an end, leading through a variable sequence from initiation to resolution. Why, then, can this phenomenon also be referred to as a social *force*? The reason for this dual identification is that while momentum refers to a certain behavioral form that people attain as they experience the ongoing flow of life (a process), it also signifies the impetus, thrust, and power displayed by those possessing it (force). Moreover, it is a highly complex and intricate phenomenon, rooted deeply at the core of people's sensations of feeling, energy, and existence. The following series of discussions probes into several depth dimensions of momentum, focusing on various aspects of its nature.

Humans and Objects

The natural sciences offer some profound insights into the ontological essence of motion: its fundamental source forces governing its sustenance and change, and its impact through the process of collision. Yet basic distinctions between objects and human beings raise questions about the suitability of physical-science formulations to the present study.

Upon consideration, several areas of convergence emerge, bespeaking the value of comparing these two realms. Galileo's work, outlining the laws of motion operating under vacuum conditions, led to Newtonian inertia theory which held that both movement and its stationary antithesis will continue unabated unless forcibly disturbed. From this base we can posit a *principle of social inertia*: In order to change one's state or rate of movement, a pulse of energy from some source is needed. This is not to say that humans are a static species, immobile and unevolving, but rather that the natural tendency to continue existing in a comfortable routine (rut) must first be overcome for the dynamic fluctuation of momentum to occur. Resistance forces, pressing for retention of the status quo, are then recognizable in an array of social and psychological procrastinations and impediments. Such barriers, found at both the onset and the termination of the momentum sequence (as we will see in affective relationships) as well as throughout, provide a "friction" that makes change require effort. This form of inertial proclivity finds its epitome in the case of zero momentum, where the will to advance is met by an equal amount of stabilization pressure, holding performative level constant.

The present conception of *impetus* or *carry-through* is also paralleled by Leibniz's theories on primitive and derivative force. Leibniz proposed that a powerful thrust can lead to associated secondary propulsions, which has been refined and explained here as resulting from the circular feedback process. Early behavioral impetus is returned through a tripartite reaction system (cognitive, emotional, and physiological) to generate recycled impulse, eventually cresting in the carry-through motion.

A third similarity concerns the existence of *natural ceiling levels* of performance for humans and objects. Newton's experiments led him to postulate a maximum rate of terminal velocity beyond which falling bodies cannot accelerate. These observations, extrapolated to the social world, suggest that behavioral peaks, varying with the individual and activity, emerge to produce the plateau or "cruising" phase of the momentum experience. Thus, limits are inherent in the performance of both human beings and inanimate things.

However, attributing the properties of objects to people is necessarily limited, given the quintessential differences in their basic natures. Contradictions are largely attributable to divergences in their fundamental origin, or source of motion. Many conflicting theories have been advanced by natural scientists to explain the ultimate cause of mobility in the universe: Pre-Socratic philosophers pondered the possibility of an unknown, quasi-living force in nature; Aristotle wrote of elements seeking their "natural" place; and modern physicists consider objects fundamentally immobile (capable of shedding inertia only through interaction with moving objects). People, in contrast, are clearly able to inaugurate locomotion at will. The repercussions of this distinction are wide-ranging, especially in terms of humans' and objects' respective momentum-generating capacities. While objects must wait passively for their environment to act on them (in moving, changing direction, or coming to a halt), humans can aggressively become motivated, plot a course, and reach an objective.

A further disparity, related to this, concerns Descartes' law of *conservation of momentum*, which asserts that a collision between two bodies will preserve the total sum of their previous momenta (although perhaps realigning it). Objects, as reactors, are incapable of introducing added propulsion into encounters and, as such, must engage each other within the confines of previously flowing energy. One body may gain force but only at the expense of the other. Humans, with their ability to create thrust, are not bound by this principle of conservation. In fact, the opposite tendency prevails: Social interaction fosters an overall momentum upheaval. A high degree of dynamic impetus is usually transmitted among parties (as seen in the contagion of collective behavior), often producing gains in intensity for the entire group through circular reaction. Similarly, depression and the frustration of counterproductivity can spread from social contact, leaving all participants more stymied and debilitated.

In sum, a flexible, open-minded comparison to the physical sciences can yield great benefits for social-sciences analysis, producing an opportunity to learn about the phenomena under study through both their convergences and divergences.

Momentum and the Self

Human existence comprises a continuous, concurrent negotiation of many spheres of life. We all relate to these diverse parts of our lives with varying attitudes, feelings, and approaches. As seminal philosophers, psychologists and sociologists of the humanistic tradition have long maintained,[2] the human self is composed of a variety of facets, or roles, that are specialized to represent the complete individual in each recurrent social situation. James (1890) was the first to write of this multiple realities phenomenon, holding that diverse, even conflicting, perceptions of people should be accepted as subjectively based and therefore not governed by the criteria of objective evaluation. He wrote that a man "has as many social selves as there are distinct groups of persons about whose opinions he cares" (1890:374). Schutz (1967)[3] carried this one step further, claiming that we can only experience or "interlock streams of consciousness" with another person along one dimension of his or her character. Each person thus maintains an "inner life" that remains totally private and transcends all of these diverse forms of consciousness. Mead (1934) went on to apply his own terminology to this concept of the fragmented personality, referring to the various roles that people assume for each concrete setting as "me's" and the central, underlying part of the self as the "I." Thus, in shifting from one sphere of life to another we abandon and adopt a new set of ambitions and concerns, but the *core self* (Mead's "I" and Schutz's "inner life") remains constant, binding these multiple selves together and providing continuity of identity.

Each sphere of life reflects upon this central identity through its contribution to the individual's self-image and ego, affecting confidence and the willingness to take risks which may evoke momentum. These are stratified in importance, however, with some more centrally lodged than others. Performance in a high-ranking dimension, such as affective relationships or career achievement, can have greater influence on one's self-impression than one situated low on the hierarchy, such as group solidarity.[4]

The interrelation of spheres is basically indirect, through their influence on the core self and its reciprocal reinspiration and reinfusion of each with energy.[5] Sometimes a powerful negative momentum in one area can have a draining effect on all others, siphoning off attention and effort they would normally receive. According to the cue utilization hypothesis (Easterbrook, 1959), the human organism is incapable of simultaneously processing too many stimuli. Thus an excess from one sphere overburdens others. An emotional "black hole" is thereby created, emptying the individual of all energy produced. Inversely, when the momentum generated in one sphere is overwhelmingly positive, it can spill over into the others. We can all recollect the "Midas touch" sensation of everything going right, where a feeling of buoyancy prevails due to simultaneous peaking in multiple spheres.

The accumulated sum of positive and negative momenta from all spheres then becomes the *compound momentum*, or prevailing velocity of the central, core self. This can vary with situational events, immediate surroundings (eliciting the dominance of one sphere), relation to long-range goals, or the nature of each individual's personality (incorporating different capacities for momentum). Major events can become enduring overall momentum makers or breakers through the overwhelmingly powerful impulse they create, setting in motion such a strong rhythmic life force that individuals are either uplifted to the core or totally debilitated.[6] Deaths of loved ones can have such a demoralizing effect, forever disabling some from achieving the preset necessary to momentum, while well-timed wealth or fame can launch others onto a path guaranteeing permanent success.

A significant note in this regard concerns momentum's effect on the quality of life. Beyond opportunities for instrumental success, momentum's presence can mean the difference between an existence of ennui and one of high drama. Without it one may toil drudgingly at both work and leisure, beset by an experience so banally mundane that neither highs nor lows are discovered. In contrast, risking failure in an attempt to challenge victory produces exhilaration. Some people, in fact, purposefully seek momentum for this reason alone.[7]

To recapitulate, discrete spheres of life are capable of encountering the ebb and flow of momentum through the individual's actions both alone and in concert with others. But this mercurial force does not remain isolated in the periphery; it flows instead into the central core self and affects the entire individual. Recirculating distribution then carries the power or privation into all the social selves, completing the interrelational feedback process.

Environmental Influences

While factors internal to individuals and groups can affect their development of momentum, external framing features of the social world also have great influence. This discussion focuses on characteristics of the social environment and the role they play in stimulating, reinforcing, or dampening momentum.

On the grandest scale, essential qualities of the macro *structural setting* frame momentum and its components. Cultural and national location can contribute positively or adversely to the creation of a social milieu where momentum can incubate and thrive. National character, determining those goals and values societally emphasized, affects the mode of activities pursued by the majority of people and, in subtle although pervasive ways, the common personality framework internalized by many through socialization (Veroff et al., 1960, 1962; McClelland, 1961). These intangible social norms, customs, and temperaments may be reinforced in their effects on momentum by concrete physical characteristics found in particular locales, such as geographic terrain or climate (McClelland, 1961; Jokl, 1964). For example, colder countries with religious, familial, and historical traditions that emphasize hard work, compounded by heavily ingrained achievement and success orientations (such as Germany), will most likely see a profusion of momenta generated along instrumental, task-related veins. The warmer Latin countries, in contrast, are known for their propensity toward momentum in lurid love affairs and a more easy-going attitude toward work. The exact validity of these cultural stereotypes is secondary to the main point, that the structural ambiance produced through a combination of national, cultural, and physical attributes may influence the strength of momentum's motivational and arousal components, affect the time of year in which it is most likely to flourish, and specify the type of behavior into which performative intensity is channeled.

Contributions from the *organizational setting* constitute the next most immediate bracket of human behavior. Included herein is the general field or area where momentum occurs and the type of formal organization (if any) further shaping its environment. Considerably more specific than the preceding domain, the propulsions and restrictions of decreed rules and regulations customarily replace the broader guidelines of inculcated norms and mores. Consistent with my discussion of careers (Chapter 5), a continuum of control may be exerted by environments, ranging from those whose loose, uninhibiting nature leaves the individual unrestricted to follow whatever inclination emerges as inspirational (e.g., the arts), to areas where behavioral expectations are so firmly defined that only a single allocated route is tolerated (e.g., the military). The latter structure crushes goals that may inadvertently arise situationally, as well as hampering the flow of arousal and emotions outside officially sanctioned activities, thus stifling momentum toward ends other than those formally encouraged. In contrast, less controlled institutions and fields offer the freedom to develop intensity in creative expression but lack the pressure and central focus that some individuals need to become motivated. A final significant dimension concerns the competitive backdrop for momentum, or the number of bodies set in opposition over the same goals. In zero-sum situations where two or more parties vie directly for limited rewards, tension provokes a rise in arousal and emotional excitement. Other areas relying largely on inner direction encourage a strengthening of self-motivation and drive. This diversity in stimulation (arousal) affects people differently, some crumbling and others thriving, according to their personalities, their familiarity with the experience, and the momentum needs of their particular activities.

On the micro interactional level, *social networks* provide an informal backdrop for productive enterprises. Here, constraints are formed less by abstract understandings than by the specific characteristics of others in the social grouping. As portrayed in military units, primary groups can serve as crucial determinants of attitude and hence behavior, channeling effort and aspiration toward some goals and away from others (see Moskos, 1970; Little, 1948; Shils and Janowitz, 1948). Interpersonal norms, often guided by one particularly charismatic figure, can encourage or discourage the summoning of energy to foster creation and overcome inertia. Occasionally the mere presence of others provokes arousal and aids momentum, according to social facilitation (Zajonc, 1965). Social aggregates, beyond being driven mutually to impress, can create a climate where each person utilizes the others for support and stimulation, thereby aiding the destruction of inertial force and providing joint inspiration. Depending on the size of the collectivity, momentum can be particularly aided at varying stages of development. Lone individuals have an advantage in getting started because they encounter the least combined inertial resistance pressure and have only their own actions to coordinate in launching activity. Crowds are favored for building intensity because of the excitement generated by continuous interpersonal contact. Masses are most adapted to maintaining momentum, since once a flowing motion has gripped such a large, diversified body of unconnected individuals, it will be sustained by the same self-interest that initially led them to it. Therefore, mass movements, slow to develop and spread, often retain their momentum the longest through the principle of inertial conservation.

Time bounding, another structural constraint, shapes momentum more abstractly. Activities and spheres vary in their degree of temporal determinacy, some having strict confinements while others are potentially unlimited. While overall restriction or its lack cannot be directly related to performance, the degree of bounding, when present, is influential. To wit, the addition of time pressure can intensify effort and behavioral outcome, making episodic affairs more passionate than enduring association, and athletic events facing enormous anticipatory build-up for a short survival span more heated and swift than wars of extended duration. Thus, the long-short dimension produces a continuum with a built-in provlicity for momentum toward either end.

Hence, the various types of environments that constitute momentum's context of occurrence have marked but differing effects on the behavior transpiring within them. National and cultural structures affect the preparation phase of momentum the most, influencing the sorts of goals that will be sought and the planning of routes to attain them. Social networks have their biggest input in the impulse phase, affecting the mood, energization, and decision-making of momentum candidates through daily encounters with them. Organizational settings make their presence felt most strongly during the carry-through phase, reinforcing or destroying supplemental efforts toward the goal, depending on its convergence with official or normative policy. Finally, time bounding affects the entire process because of its implications for the denouement phase, giving a vibrant urgency to short-duration projects and sapping the intensity from seemingly interminable undertakings.

Relation of Force to Momentum

I have postulated throughout this examination of momentum that there is a fundamental dynamic process underlying the generation and regeneration of movement, monitoring human behavior through the various stages of intensity, and modulating the available energy, effort, and ability into diverse degrees of productive output. This operates, though, on a *sliding* scale, as we note that the amount of raw force (arousal) exerted creates different levels of productive intensity (performance) along evolving points of the momentum sequence.

For example, the early stages of initiation, where anticipation, visualizing, and preparation occur, can be characterized by high degrees of motivation, drive, arousal, and exertion without yielding commensurate, tangible results. This condition of *"spinning one's wheels"* is partly due to the resistance force present at this (or any) stage. Thus, where we see barriers (e.g., at the beginnings and ends of relationships or from buying and selling pressure in the stock market), discernible movement (momentum) may appear unrelated to internal push (force). The extreme of this tendency is manifested in zero momentum, where no progress occurs.

Peak momentum periods, in contrast, are characterized by an "economy of force," where efficiency is so paramount that materials are utilized to maximum potential. In this *"cruising"* stage a near equalization of effort and productivity is achieved, where the system of circular feedback recycles output to augment fresh input. Here, a moderately strong level of force generates a momentum that is relatively easy to sustain.

Upon nearing completion, however, the ratio reverses and force declines in the face of a barreling momentum "coasting" down the "home stretch." By this time, exertion may start to slacken because of the natural letdown of being nearly at the goal, and fresh force output diminishes. However, the energy return system established during the escalating phase and the excitement of anticipated achievement continue to propel behavioral intensity, so that momentum remains high. This stage, therefore, sees the greatest proportionate production of movement from the smallest amount of freshly expended might.

If we want to examine the abstract relationship between force exerted and momentum attained we may take the drive theory

TABLE 1: The Relation of Force to Momentum

Momentum = Force × Conversion Ratio

Momentum = (Primitive Force + Derivative Force − Resistance Force) × Conversion Ratio

Rate of movement	Raw inner exertion of energy	Recycled feedback	Impediments of motion	Ability to transform
		+		
Quality of performance		Future anticipation of satisfaction (confidence)	Physical, psychological, interpersonal, and structural	Inner "Gear ratio"
		or		
Level of intensity		Frustration (demoralization)	Inertia and restraint	Skill, experience, learned responses, habit, talent

of arousal (Spence and Spence, 1966) as a point of departure: To wit, performance equals the product of drive and habit. Adapting this to the present purpose, we find an individual or collective's momentum equivalent to the combined interaction between however much force can be applied and the ability to utilize and transform it into something tangible. Expanding this into more conceptually useful detail, we have the complete formula presented in Table 1.

Clearly, this portrays a complex scheme of interaction between the person's internal elements and the environment, as befits the intricate and varied nature of human situational responses.[8] A multiplicity of changing factors influence the evolution of momentum, feeding into the total picture through any one of the above variables. Thus, any unique instance and circumstance can be accommodated through modification of one or more components, producing differences in the sequence of dynamic unfolding.

Primitive force, the fresh impulse emitted through the individual's drive or desire for propulsion, usually starts out strong, invigorated by the ideals inspired from recent contact with the source of motivation. Straining to draw the complete self into action, it sustains a high intensity during the climbing and cruising stages of development. In some cases primitive force may fade toward the end, but this is not always so, as other instances contain a strong finish, spurred to the last by total exertion.

Derivative force is a delicately combined response to past and future occurrences. Both perception-evaluation and anticipation are coordinated herein, contributing in fluctuating strengths according to a person's location along the momentum sequence. Near the onset of an undertaking, the power generated by anticipation will be great while the rewards from creative achievement are still minimal. As the entire behavior progresses toward its conclusion, however, this relationship reverses itself, anticipatory energy becoming increasingly replaced by thrust from the perception, feedback, and evaluation of concrete production, now yielding the greater impetus. Like the other components, derivative force mutates according to the social meaning accorded it in the particular activity and type of situation involved. Three distinct patterns can be noted: (1) In the stock market (Chapter 4) we observe the prevalence of *discounting*, where performative level is extremely sensitive to expected events, waxing and waning from this overwhelming anticipation effect. (2) The realm of task accomplishment (Chapter 5) displays a *lag effect*, where the results of effort are only felt after the delay of an incubation period. (3) Affective relationships (Chapter 5) show us the extreme sensitivity surrounding *simultaneous reward*, the responses to hopes, dreams, and actions being nearly instantaneously reflected in the quality of the bond. Any one of these models, to differing degrees, can be injected into the momentum equation as a result of its emergence in the feedback-expectation system.

Resistance force can originate within a plethora of obstacles, diverging in composition from the totally abstract to the inescapably concrete and exerting a continuum of perceived opposition to progress from token to insurmountable. Highly dependent on situational surroundings, this component can play an active or passive role, being lodged either within or outside the individual, group, or social object. Generally at a maximum near the beginning, it weakens once movement commences, although it is capable of being resurrected in full power by outside stimuli at any time.[9]

Conversion ratio, perhaps the most intricate element here, consists of the individual or group's internal level of productivity, and their ability to utilize the force provided and create concrete thrust from it. The quality or level at which this variable ratio operates determines the amount of output that will result from a given degree of input in much the same way that an automobile's gear mechanism mediates between the engine's revolutions and those of the wheels. Like a car, people approach an endeavor in low gear, eventually shifting into higher ratios as they warm up and accelerate their velocity. In humans (and associated institutions) this transformational capacity can be affected by several factors. One's skill at the activity in question, arising through a combination of talent and experience, sets the quality of dominant response patterns that will emerge when energy is applied. While natural ability is innately fixed within each individual, acquired competence can fluctuate due to repetitively derived familiarity with a field or even over the course of a single protracted involvement. As habits become ingrained, the conversion ratio escalates, increasing the efficiency of operation. Enterprises involving a high degree of difficulty or uncertainty may always remain low in this regard. Thus, we glimpse the inner working of the dynamic behavioral system, which illustrates some reasons underlying the wide performance gap between novices and experts.

Reservoirs of Power

All organisms maintain inner reserves of somatic and psychic energy that are available to the body in times of emergency (Cannon, 1929). When pressing needs such as basic survival, emotional well-being, or endurance beyond physical exhaustion arise, a release mechanism is triggered, removing the barrier between mundane everyday resources and these special reservoirs. My own personal observation and experiences supplement the academic physiological belief that perception is highly influential in setting the limits of exertion, gauging how tired people feel and how far they can go. The same amount of effort can therefore vary in the exhaustion it produces, depending on people's general mental set and particular thoughts at the time, so that a constant output can fluctuate between being draining, tolerable, and refreshing. Since momentum is so heavily tied to reservoirs of power through their storage of raw force, let us examine the major circumstances under which this inner barrier is pierced.

On rare, often dramatic occasions, there is a sharp breakthrough that appears as a flash and lasts only briefly. This can be attributed to the *startle effect*, where someone who is engaged in an activity suddenly becomes infused with power, leaping to heights of performance hitherto unattainable through a charismatic inner thrust or surprising external occurrence. Inspiration can stem from disaster (threat of life to oneself or another), to shock (an unexpected loud noise), to an intense, overwhelming desire.[10] This demonstrates in a climactic way that the boundaries of human capacity are largely unknown.

More common is the *remomentum* phenomenon, where an outpouring of power surges as the end draws near. Soldiers described the feeling of being abruptly lifted from the fatigue and depression of combat by knowing they would soon be relieved, finding themselves able to exert more effort into the fighting than previously. Marathoners regularly encounter this experience as they go into their "kick" toward the finish, throwing their last stores of energy to work. In this form, then, the pressure of a natural stopping point serves to inspire the release of reserved energy, regardless of the person's current condition.[11]

Thirdly there is the outpouring of inner reservoirs accompanying the *second wind*. Evoked under quite different circumstances, this release of inner barriers comes only at the point of total routinization and exhaustion, after the immediate supply of energy is depleted and behavior has sunk into a rut. Having run, fought, concentrated, or consoled for a long time, one becomes bodily and mentally weary and begins to feel unable to push onward. Performance starts to dip, emotions to lag, and stamina to crumble as one continues to forge ahead, albeit at a lesser rate. Then, suddenly, a flood of fresh energy is perceived to appear, invigorating the entire self and boosting momentum to higher levels than ever before achieved. Distinctly unlike making a fresh start, the second wind need not include the early problems associated with overcoming inertia, warming up, or establishing rhythmicity; instead, it boosts performance immediately to a superior plateau of ease and fluidity.

The similarities linking these three forms of power underscore their overlaps and their relation to inner energy stores. But major differences also exist, accounting for the diverse conditions producing them and their unique natures. Drawing on the formula relating force to momentum, we can see that each of these three traces its onset to a separate component in the equation. The startle effect is fundamentally a giant adrenaline rush, enabling astounding behavioral feats. This is rooted in primitive force, or the basic impulse of energy emitted from within. A remomentum is causally connected with the approaching end and the anticipation of rest once there, signaling to the self that those last grains of strength held in reserve can be released now, as they will be replenished shortly. Hence this final push involves a primarily conscious adjustment that stimulates greater yield from the derivative force. The second wind also stems from an adjustment, but it concerns the conversion ratio rather than psychological perception. Having expended superficially available strength but still pressing forward, the individual effects a jump into higher gear, eliciting greater strength from diminished exertion. At the same time, the demand to continue causes a release of reserved power that flows through the primitive force channels, fueling the new conversion ratio into action. Thus, like an automobile, there is the pause of exhaustion that neutralizes the gears, and then the kick into overdrive with the flooding of new force.

COMPONENTIAL ANALYSIS OF MOMENTUM

Having examined the components and types of momentum in an isolated manner, let me now integrate them into a working processual model that shows their roles and interrelations. The ensuing discussion will delve into fundamental characteristics and dynamics of this spiraling process to offer insight into its origin and universal symmetry of form.

Throughout this chapter I have indicated that there are several key components necessary for the rise of momentum. Exactly how do all these constituent parts fit together to form the blueprint for momentum? Let us consider an abstract model representing the most generic image of this adaptable process, from its utilization of contributing components to the detailed sequence of development comprising its rise, feedback, and dissolution, as shown in Figure 1.

Figure 1 describes the placement and role of all the fundamental elements and dynamics of the momentum spiral. As we have seen, *goal*-oriented behavior is key to momentum. The vision of a goal, arising from any of several spheres, serves as the central inspiration that binds and impels the entire vortex of subsequent behavior. Goals also perform the vital function of defining the direction toward which people strive. Holding constant as ideal stimulations to creative activity, goals identify the relative progress, stagnation, and/or negative slippage that has been attained throughout the entire quest and serve as partial performance yardsticks.

For the purpose of this analysis, however, I will consider goals as outside the momentum process. Whether they derive from the realm of internal biological needs (drives) or from external cultural values (incentives), they must first be recognized and accepted through a conscious *motivation* process before they can become sought-after ideals. The rise of motivation to pursue a potential goal is highly influenced by the individual or group's current social, psychological, and physical readiness; with life saturated by multifarious involvements, commitments, and satisfactions, people are unlikely either actively to seek or eagerly to accept a goal presented to them.

Motivation can also be affected by structural and organizational features of the surrounding social situation, being facilitated by other dynamic activities and the absence of restricting encumbrances. When open to new horizons or surrounded by favorable circumstances, however, people will often readily become excited by indications of a particular activity's promise, invoking the psychic, social, and somatic energy to devote to a challenging crusade. Beyond inner drives and cultural incentives, motivations can arise situationally, suggested to people by something they see, hear, or do. Action-induced motivation usually develops when a goal inadvertently evolves out of behavior that is initially nonpurposive. Here, an activity undertaken for intrinsic enjoyment can serendipitously become transformed by a side dimension that blossoms into compelling focus and forges unanticipated velocity (either up or down) almost before the transfer of attention is noticed. For example, instances of collective behavior are often launched spontaneously with a group of people who find themselves together, begin to interact and become excited, and work themselves into a fully aimed motivation that leads them through the complete momentum cycle.

Perceiving, evaluating, and internalizing one of the various motivational pressures then stirs the inner will to achieve the goal selected. People begin concentrating their attention and energy on moving toward that end, strengthening the desire or need for its attainment. The conscious thinking process continues as the goal is subjectively internalized, analyzed, and plotted. Mulling over the entire project, people fantasize alternatively between the delights of eventually experiencing the desired objective and the dreaded agonies potentially located in the toil, frustration, and obstacles to achievement. Plans of action are formulated, rejected, and modified in anticipation of the future. Thus, at this point, people begin reacting to the possible scenarios suggested by the goal in a primarily mentalistic mode, evoking a host of related reactions.

First among these are the less rational sensations arising from the *emotional* domain. The ascendance of a motivational drive

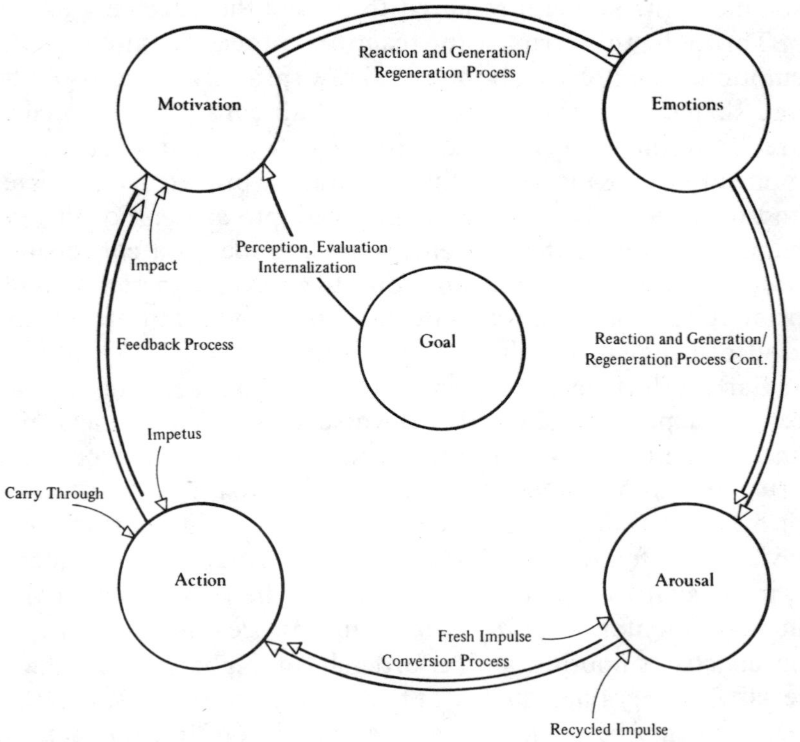

Figure 1 Cross-Sectional Model of Momentum

and its accompanying vision of the goal spark an abundance of feelings centering on both the perception and internalization already accomplished, and on the visualization of potential future developments. Strong responses are often evoked, which well up inside people, filling them with voluminous but sometimes conflicting irrational and impulsive sentiments that will soon spill over into propulsion.

Heightened emotions and intellectual stimulation, in turn, incite a rise in *arousal* level. Their imaginations abuzz with activated fervor, people transmit sensory messages throughout the body, generating physiological responses (i.e., adrenalin rush, increased respiration, and heart rate). Generally, this constitutes the physical and psychological intensification that summons the strength required to pursue the selected goal.

Through this tripartite reaction process (intellectual, emotional, and physical) the initial raw (primitive) force is built and shaped (generation process) until all constituent elements are combined to form an *impulse*, or inner thrust, to momentum. At this point the preparation process is complete and the impulse is ready to be launched into *action*. For this to happen, however, the raw energy must undergo a conversion process where the person's or collective's skill, experience, and prior state of motion (breakdown of immobility) influence the kind of behavior capable of being produced.

Early efforts are frequently unrewarding because of the resistance pressure of inertia (or worse, of negative momentum) and unfamiliarity with the task (due to lack of knowledge or "rustiness"). Action occurring during this first spiral is directed primarily toward overcoming impediments to motion and laying the foundation for the achievements of subsequent spirals. Learned response patterns must be carved out of the human potential, creating mental and physical habits that can be enacted smoothly and effortlessly at higher performance levels. The ingrained quality of these dominant responses marks the difference between early and later phases of the momentum sequence and, more broadly, between the novice and the expert operator. Thus, during this initial spiral, behavior is choppy and heavily reliant on continual act-related thinking.

Once the energetic thrust of internal impulse has been converted into an outward behavioral manifestation, *impetus* is created. This is the initial display of the creative inner turbulence, resulting in first interaction with the external environment. Reverberations of the active impetus ripple outward, affecting all those contacted. Those others, in turn, react to the deed performed, triggering the feedback process. The action's *impact*, or effect, is made known to its makers through self-reflection, and as friends, colleagues, and acquaintances impart their responses or give subtler demonstrative indications. Unless people perceive the effects of their actions, they accord little symbolic meaning to the experience they have undergone and fail to complete the cycle which leads to momentum. But when behavioral results are acknowledged and favorably appraised, energy is recycled into remotivation, the point of primal origin, the cycle is conceptually complete and people are ready to begin again, entering the second spiral. Neither a static nor limited process, momentum continues its charged rise in a circular fashion through this *return, feedback,* and *recommencement.*

In the succeeding componential spiral the conscious motivational process is once again called forth to evaluate the results of efforts thus far expended and to reflect on the needs or incentives powering the initial thrust to the goal. The importance of the chosen aim must be reaffirmed, along with a continuing commitment to its pursuit. Each individual involved thus faces the personal challenge of deciding again whether his or her dedication is adequate to maintain the initial aspiration in light of difficulties and uncertainties encountered. Perseverance, that dogged determination to strive on despite setbacks, is an important character trait enhancing people's motivational, and hence their momentum, potential. "Achievement motivation," also referred to as the need to achieve, can enhance the likelihood of a sustained rational thrust toward the selected end (see Atkinson, 1964, 1968; McClelland, 1961).

When joined by a resurgence of emotional and arousal reinspiration, the three elements combine to forge a new generation of *fresh impulse* (primitive force). Beyond this fundamentally simple repetition of the preceding functions, the second cycle, as differentiated from the first, assumes the role of reactor to recent achievements. Hence, people must respond, first through motivation and then through emotions and arousal to the behavior created and the impact it has had on both themselves and others. The motivational process, moreover, also serves in these succeeding spirals to direct and channel previously evoked energy and action along the selected path toward the goal.

When the reaction process produces satisfaction and confidence, an upward spiraling motion ensues, but when reflectivity results in disappointingly negative feedback, the process can easily reverse, creating a dramatically plummeting disaster characterized by insecurity and despair. It is significant to note that in all cases recycled impulse is generated by a *like* response from colleagues and self, predominantly positive appraisal begetting positive impetus and negative the reverse.[12] This supplemental force occurring contemporaneous to reinspiration constitutes *recycled impulse* (derivative force). Thus, we see here the internally self-generating system at work, where people absorb others' responses to actions produced and transform them into usable, practical resources. The feedback mechanism completes the final link, trapping and returning each formulation of inner thrust for reuse, losing only that propulsion which erodes due to the "friction" forces of natural resistance inherent in everyday life. In this way, a cumulative effect of ever-mounting power and intensity is achieved.

Encountering the conversion process, the preceding achievements become especially significant, as the gear ratio shifts to a more productive proportion due to the inertial breakdown and accumulation of skill and experience. Finally we have a recurrence of action, sliding along with a somewhat smoother rhythm and greater efficiency as a result of the previous internal preparation. Successfully effecting a second instance of behavioral impetus that proceeds beyond its predecessors constitutes another symbolic accomplishment. At last one capitalizes on the impact resulting from initial inspiration through a recurrence of effort in the same vein. Redirecting activity toward this common end engenders a *carry-through* powered by the combined fresh and recycled impulses, capturing a fleeting, knife-edged spurt and anchoring it into tangible, enduring solidity. Realizing this sole remaining component seals the entire process definitionally, ensuring the existence of a true momentum with all the recognizable characteristics.

Picked up once more by the feedback mechanism, these achievements are again returned for cognitive appraisal, starting the whole process into another of the continually ascending spiraling motions. Each new cycle thereafter basically resembles the second in form, as it has a foundation upon which to build and regenerate intensity. After a while, as the person becomes more familiar with the necessary motor skills, conscious reflection diminishes, replaced by habituation and confidence. Performative level can thus climb according to the dictates of personal, situational, and structural conditions.

Clearly, more than one mode of this escalation exists in the empirical world, especially regarding the speed of acceleration to the peak. A *continuum of onset,* providing the flexibility integral to any model of human behavior, ensures that each case proceeds through the spiraling process at its own rhythm and pace. Gradual starts follow a leisurely and sedate path effecting a relative extension and separation of the stages, while a whirlwind motion that telescopes progression, often causing componential overlapping and condensation, portrays the spark start.

The *spread of momentum* from one individual to another can also follow diverse patterns. Depending on the type of group and the related bonds connecting the associated people, there are two forms this process can take. Tightly knit groupings with a high degree of self-immersion in the collective whole (small groups, crowds) usually manifest the *unified* form of contagion. Here, the entire assemblage (e.g., a ball team) undergoes the experience as one, passing from one stage to the next and carrying out the spiraling process together. New members are pulled into the midst of this eddy and swiftly integrated into the greater momentum. By contrast, settings where discrete autonomy and preservation of self are normally maintained display the *differentiated* form of dispersion (masses). Carefully visually monitoring each other, the myriad individuals are separately undergoing their own inner spirals. Fairly equal synchrony is maintained through the "bump effect" of transmission, as people push each other to intensification through increasingly frenetic and haphazard contact. This is analogous to the kinetic theory of gasses and matter, which views all vaporous or solid objects (e.g., the mass) as composed of small particles enjoined in random motion. Total velocity, or temperature, then results from the combined effects of all particles' individual speeds and the impact of their frequent collisions, as we will see in the stock market.

When escalation has leveled off and the plateauing period draws to an end, we witness the *decline in momentum*. People's momentum deintensifications follow a format similar to their ascending counterpart as the spiraling process continues to revolve through all the fundamental components. However, instead of being spurred to greater arousal and emotional heights by noetic reflection, people are relaxed into passivity. Each motivational appraisal initiates a diminishing velocity through its evaluation of performance quality and the dwindling degree of inspiration evoked by the goal. A conscious or unconscious decision to reduce thrust can arise from a variety of conditions: (1) Momentum can be suddenly broken by an outside force; (2) after repeated attempts, achieving the desired end may be adjudged impossible and further effort suspended; (3) although cognizant that the aim is attainable, the pursuers may lose interest in the pursuit and decide to abandon the quest; (4) hailing the goal within sight, people may reduce their output of effort (letdown) and coast to the finish without overly straining their remaining resources; or (5) the energy summoned may be released in a huge sigh of relief upon attainment of the end. Here, as before, the variance between the span of time utilized and rate of deceleration can encompass a wide magnitude. Gradually gliding to a conclusion keeps the sequence of components orderly and distinct. Effecting a sudden cessation collapses the process into a narrower spiral with a steeper angle of descent. Abrupt and instantaneous loss of momentum transforms the downward cycling into a straight line that immediately deflates like a punctured balloon.

We note, therefore, a great *diversity in conclusion* concerning momentum's manner of approaching the end and its level of strength upon reaching the goal. A task's consummation may find those involved on a forceful, excited high, having maintained intensity throughout due to compelling internal motivation or outside pressure not to slacken (i.e., from a time deadline). Finales with verve are also generated by a concluding remomentum, or the outpouring of withheld reserves in a last, all-out, exhilarative "kick." Some resolutions display a return to calm inertia whence activity sprang; the "petering out" format represents a gradual overwhelming by this kind of quiescence, or passivity can arrive suddenly through the precipitous drop that leaves a participant "cold" (e.g., when momentum is stolen or destroyed by a competitor). Last, at the point of momentum's expiration, the associated individuals may have descended past the neutral state to a nadir of performance and intensity level. Unpleasant obstacles that stall a project just short of the finish sap energy and enthusiasm, leaving frustration and weary depression. Even worse, a sharpening of destructive force is sometimes required to attain freedom (e.g., cutting the cord of strong affective bonds), forcing actors into aggressively negative velocity from which they emerge tense and unhappy.

Negative Momentum

The *negative* counterpart of this upward spiral is similar to it in form, although distinguished by different characteristics. The early part of the negative process is essentially the same, including the importance of internal and external receptivity to the goal, the rise of motivation through a conscious assessment of needs and values, and the associated intensification of emotion and arousal in preparation to act. The *start* to misfortune that may eventually develop into a catastrophic trend can occur in any one of three manners: through a clear breakdown or failure in the actual implementation of the plans, through a disappointed self-perception and evaluation of the actions undertaken, or through a negative reaction by others to the behavior produced. Thus, the divergence from the positive momentum pattern can be rooted either in the conversion process where the impulse is transformed into the capability for action, in the performance process where the action is solidified, or in the feedback process where unsatisfactory appraisals of the behavior can cause dejection, frustration, and loss of confidence.

In some instances the feeling of negativity can be overcome by dominant underlying sensations of hope, calm, confidence, continuingly strong motivation, and a foundation of past success. Where these are shaky and self-assurance is insecure, however, the positive outlook can crumble and a fear of the future replace it. Then, as noted earlier, the negative feedback generates further negative impulses and the second spiral (carry-through) continues the downward trend initiated by the first. This can occur in two ways: Either the "heart" or visceral thrust of motivation, emotion, and arousal may be somehow diminished by the poor past performance, producing an impetus that is inadequate to achieving positive success and only aids the worsening process, or brash effort may be made to recoup previous losses, resulting in an overabundance of effort that is insufficiently planned or controlled and results in worse damage. We see instances of the first form of negative momentum carry-through in a team of chronic losers who have so little confidence in themselves that the first setback they encounter leads them to the immediate conclusion that their chances of winning are lost; thus they forfeit their ability to evoke enough impulse to propel themselves forward (toward their goal). The second type of negative momentum accelaration can be exemplified by racetrack gamblers who try to regain the money they have already squandered by betting on long shots and hoping for the big payoffs; this abandonment of solid, reliable strategy in favor of recklessness only intensifies the movement into a reverse spiral.

Once anchored negatively by one or a combination of these processes, the subsequent spirals evolve through similar patterns, plummeting those caught in the demoralizing whirlwind of frustration and fatality to even lower ebbs. The momentum may stay confined to those who initiated it, but unlike its positive inverse, it is highly infectious. Negative propulsion can *spread* to people who try to help those afflicted with misfortune, dragging them into the sinking state as well, or it can engulf those who inadvertently wander too near the source of the disaster cycle, adding their weight to the burgeoning negativity.

The *conclusion* to this horribly charged life force can also follow a variety of modes. Sudden ends, where the declining parties are swiftly lifted out of the depths into neutrality or a positive impetus, are rare. As the stock market shows, it is much easier to lose confidence quickly than it is to rebuild it. Thus, when negative momentum reverses itself sharply, this can usually be traced to the influence of outside factors, such as an opponent's loss of momentum or a change in the definition or perception of the rules, goals, or boundaries. Gradual finales are the more common, people slowly managing to regain control of their direction by overcoming their defeatist momentum before they are capable of attaining neutrality and the hope of positive impetus. This process is exceedingly difficult and requires a real inner transformation, necessitating the destruction of the established behavioral model. Some outside aid is usually necessitated for this reversal as well, at least in the very beginning. Reinforcing teams with fresh athletes or equipment can serve as such a boost, providing them with the spirit and rejuvenation to attempt playing their way out of a defeatist posture. Finally, the predominant form of negative momentum expiration occurs via a death, total defeat, or abdiction of involvement with the activity. The majority of people, once locked into a negative spiral, are unable to break out of it and seek refuge by voluntarily abandoning a doomed cause and cutting their losses, as in an unsuccessful venture. Where this is impossible or unthinkable, people continue sinking until some natural stopping point (a technical knockout in boxing or death from an illness one has been fighting) intervenes to conclude the activity, saving them from further pain and humiliation.

In sum, negative momentum follows a similar blueprint of build-up, action, feedback, evaluation, regeneration, and remobilization as its more fortunate relation, but instead of yielding positive results that bring the desired end closer, it wreaks a patterned havoc that increases the distance to the goal (regardless of whether that goal is commonly thought of as desirable or undesirable).

The basic models presented here contain the potential for adaptability to fit an infinite variety of unique sequences, personalities, situations, and settings, pressured by the needs and constraints embedded in the confronting challenge of each goal. Yet throughout this diversity, the guiding inner process maintains a constancy of form resting squarely on the synchronization of crucial components and the interrelation of subsystems. The remaining chapters will illustrate this.

NOTES

1. See Mead (1932) and Natanson (1956: 74-79) for a thorough discussion of these different states of temporal endurance and their significance.

2. See James (1890), Santayana (1922), Mead (1934), and Goffman (1959, 1961).

3. Originally published in German in 1932, under the title, *Der Sinnhafte Aufban der Sozialen Welt.*

4. According to Schutz's (1967) definition of zones of relevance, the importance of these dimensions is fluid and constantly shifting, so that a crisis in one area may temporarily bring it to the fore and cause it to have a greater influence on one's identity and self-confidence than it would ordinarily merit.

5. Occasionally a direct link will form between closely related spheres, as when a particularly brilliant task produces impetus for one's greater career, or when clever sociability aids the inception of a relationship.

6. Steve Weed, fiance to Patty Hearst at the time of her abduction, has remarked repeatedly on how that whole incident and its repercussions destroyed the momentum of his life, from which he has never been able to recover.

7. Ironically, those people who take achieving the state of momentum as their goal usually have more difficulty attaining it than do those who concentrate on a more tangible end and harness their total efforts in service of its realization. Even in a directly competitive situation where an opponent realizes that his or her adversary has the greater momentum, becoming too focused on breaking or stealing that momentum can have a deleterious effect on one's own rhythm, energy, and sense of direction, distracting concentration from the ultimate goal and "flooding out" whatever momentum one may have acquired.

8. This momentum formula stands in particular contrast to the simplicity of the equation computing momentum from the product of mass and acceleration (momentum = mass × acceleration). In that construction, the inanimate character of objects is especially assumed, their sheer presence and weight being adjudged a more important factor than their inner potential for mobility. For the interested reader who wishes to pursue further natural-science analogies to human momentum, see Atkinson (1964: 309-311).

9. Feather (1961) discusses the resistance phenomenon for goal-directed behavior, concluding that it is weakest when the probability of success is either very high or very low, and rises to greatest levels for tasks representing moderate challenges.

10. An example of the latter situation can be found in Olympic history when, during the 1968 summer competition, Bob Beamon shocked the world by long-jumping nearly two feet farther than anyone had ever done before. To this date no one has even come anywhere near this startling achievement.

11. Hull's (1932) research on maze learning, which led to the goal gradient hypothesis, supplements my present observations of humans in natural settings. In his laboratory, Hull found that rats increased their speed and level of excitement as they approached the ultimate goal.

12. This is conceptually distinct from the *cybernetic* feedback system described in theoretical engineering and adopted sociologically in Shibutani (1968) in elucidating Mead's conception of motivation. The cybernetic model measures the distance between an object or organism and the ultimate goal, being positively impelled to achievement by the frustration (negative feedback) from any difference still outstanding. Thus, the circular feedback system under discussion responds directly to the amount and type of incoming stimulation, traceable to former outgoing efforts.

3

MOMENTUM IN SPORT

More dynamically visible here than in any other social realm, the domain of sport provides an excellent arena for observing momentum. With teams sweeping up and down the field, the advantage shifting back and forth through tumultuous struggle, the fans emotionally cheering, one can hardly escape succumbing to this electrically exhilarating force. While pleasant and enthralling in the stands, momentum is paramount on the playing field. In professional sport especially, where contestants are closely matched, elements other than talent are often responsible for determining the outcome of athletic events. Dr. Thomas Tutko, professor of sport psychology, explains:

> When you're talking about high-level competition, where talent is almost equal, that little extra charge of adrenalin or motivation can be the difference between one step more and one step less [Los Angeles Times, 1978].

Precisely how is momentum characterized when removed from the abstract theoretical plane and planted in empirical

---

AUTHOR'S NOTE: This is a revised and lengthened version of a previously published article, "The Role of Momentum in Sport," by Peter Adler and Patricia A. Adler, which appeared in *Urban Life*, July 1978.

soil? Even when concretely grounded it remains an intangible element. What, then, is that extra dimension that comes alive when the physical action is pulsing? How can teams that look inferior on paper sometimes beat their supposedly more talented competitors? Statistics, although capable of relating simple victory, defeat, and concrete achievements, can never fully explain the process of personal interaction that takes place in a game (Bradley, 1976: 61); the patterned yet unpredictable nature of the human being is at issue here. This, in part, accounts for the compelling interest sport holds for millions: that unpredictability of outcome which hinges on so many nonrational and emotional factors. Momentum is but one of these constitutive forces, yet in its fullest scope, it touches nearly all of them. Concentrating on physical, intellectual, and emotional aspects, I will examine the processual life span of momentum in sport from before its inception to its final dissolution.

PREPARATION

Momentum is an *elite* form of social action; it does not come equally to all in a democratic or fair manner. People with optimal attitudes and social organization (receptivity) have a greater chance of attaining it than those who constantly complain, lag in effort, and remain aloof from cooperative ventures. Although momentum is only visible during the course of the game, factors intrinsic to its occurrence begin to build considerably before the contest begins.

Pregame

Prior to an event, athletes usually set personal *goals* toward which they will strive during the upcoming contest. Different types of goals can hinder or help athletes in their quest to achieve momentum. High aspirations often inspire players to "reach back" and produce their most substantial efforts. At other times, shifting to more limited and narrowly focused goals can help players generate a greater degree of motivation and concentration. In the latter case, momentum can be better achieved by aiming for success first in one facet of play and only later in the whole.

In either case, once goals are established, momentum then hinges on the degree of *motivation* to achieve them. Although individuals vary widely and situational factors are critical, a number of elements emerge as commonly recognized sources of inspiration.[1] From within, the drive to excel can power momentum development, as athletes seek to better their previous records. Pride can serve as another boost to impetus, helping to ensure a quality performance. External rewards also provide strong incentives to momentum-infused play, especially in the professional sports, where the extravagances of financial remuneration have been well publicized. Social status functions as a motivational force as well, since consistently superlative performance can elevate athletes to the role of cultural heroes (i.e., Muhammad Ali), bringing honor to themselves and their sex, ethnic group, race, and country. Finally, the respect of fellow athletes helps to evoke momentum, as sports circles are tightly knit and continuing employment or recruitment is highly dependent on the quality of effort and play.

Another component of the motivational readying process is the forging of psychological attitudes that will affect confidence and concentration before and during play. Players develop fears, expectations, despondency, or hopes based on how they perceive the "mental vibes" developing. A positive orientation can either smooth or block the path to momentum, depending on whether one is "psyched up" or "psyched out." Thus, even with optimally set goals and a strong motivational drive, athletes need a nurturing mental set to continue advancing through the momentum process.

Before the contest, players attempt to psych themselves up (boost their confidence) while simultaneously trying to psych out (demoralize) the opposition. Building confidence is relatively easy for those who have been successful in the past; previous winners expect to perform optimally. Their ability to carry over high-quality play from one game to the next is a clear demonstration of momentum's temporal endurance: It can be partially maintained in abeyance during time-out periods of nonplay. Familiarity with momentum also smooths the routes leading to its recurrent onset. For those who do not have a history of victory, however, the rise of confidence is problematic, and developing both it and, subsequently, momentum can be a struggle.

Many players revert to ancient superstitious traditions to overcome their fear and acquire confidence. Rituals, taboos, and fetishes have become common in sport because of the high-risk element involved there and the perceived pervasiveness of luck.[2] A range of practices fall under this category, including repeating or changing every facet of one's pregame routine to hold or cast off a spell; religiously shunning words or deeds considered forbidden; and carrying objects thought to possess special powers. These behaviors and prohibitions evolve into a set of magical mores meant to exert control over factors considered outside athletes' normal domain.

More rational, conscious machinations abound as well, as athletes fantasize about the details of their upcoming play and plot strategies for defeating specific opponents. Game plans, covering a variety of attacks and defenses to adjust to possible contingencies that may arise, are also prepared. One growing practice in this vein is visualizing: athletes carefully concentrate on imagining balls going through hoops, putts sinking into the hole, or serving for the perfect ace. No one actually knows how or why visualizing works, but its practitioners suggest that during visualizing the muscles replicate the movements that will be used later, thereby establishing ingrained motor patterns and building confidence.

In contrast to confidence is the intimidation of being psyched out over an upcoming sporting event. Often a powerful reputation built on past performances can intimidate opponents so that they feel outmaneuvered and mentally beaten before the contest begins, thereby acquiring an undesired negative momentum. Big bonuses can result if antagonists hesitate to take those extra chances that bring payoffs. In baseball this is manifested by a reluctance to steal against a good catcher or neglecting to try for an extra base against an outfielder's powerfully touted arm.

Sometimes players themselves may take an active role in trying to intimidate competitors. Through carefully managed self-presentations and occasional direct contact, they may create images of themselves to scare opposing players.

When goals are set, the effect of inspired motivations is evidenced by the individual or team's social attitude, otherwise known as *morale*. By this I refer to the dominant mental and behavioral stance taken in approaching a given endeavor: resolution, positive spirit, confidence, concentration, seriousness, self-control, and the determination to apply total effort. Without good morale, players on a team can flounder in mediocrity, unable to utilize their natural talent, incapable of experiencing the summit that comes only when all parts of the body and mind are joined and working together.

> No wonder, then, that football coaches look so eagerly for signs of *spirit, will, desire*. When teams are reasonably matched, intensity of execution makes the difference. The pain, weariness and exhaustion of the action discourage everyone. So individual morale is critical; more critical still is team morale. This is the secret behind that mystic word "momentum" so beloved by commentators [Novak, 1976: 140].

Teams that have inculcated their members with a positive joint outlook and a sense of cohesion can surpass the psychological dimension of morale to become socially psyched, or *"soced up."*[3] This incorporates both the attitudinal and associated behavioral dimensions of being collectively psyched up, and the interactional synchrony of being organizationally integrated. Shibutani (1978: 3-4) refers to a similar state in his study of military demoralization, discussing

> the degree of effectiveness with which the recognized goals of joint enterprise are pursued. . . . We are concerned with the *quality* of coordination and integration of the contributions of those who

> are involved in some kind of common endeavor. We are also concerned with *persistence* in the pursuit of collective goals—the capacity of a group to maintain its integrity and steadfastness of purpose until its objective is attained.

Teams that are "soced up" thus have in interpersonal organization conducive to the birth and diffusion of momentum: They develop it more easily from weaker impulses and anchor it more securely through a rapid contagion and an ensuing collective performance spiral.

While a person's goals, motivation, and morale can be reciprocally influential in generating spiraling motion, a variety of *emotions* also help. Hatred is one violent emotion that can reinforce motivation and help to induce subsequent physiological arousal. Players at all amateur and professional levels seem to expend more effort against rivals and disliked antagonists than against friends and comrades; they find it easier to muster the necessary aggression against repugnant or offensive opponents than against those liked or viewed neutrally. To encourage this, many coaches have instituted fines for fraternizing with opposing players.[4]

Fear, when present in moderation, can also be used to advantage by the seasoned competitor, as one football player explained:

> I think a true professional knows what to call on at every moment in the game to get charged up. When I need a booster I draw on the crowd, I draw on my pain, I draw on fear, anything. 'Cause I'm just as scared as the rest of them out there. But fear, coupled with a lot of other emotions, helps to get my mind where it needs to be.

The final element linking motivation and emotion with a momentum-filled performance is *arousal*.[5] This infusion of strength will provide the power that propels athletes to superior play. The most influential factor on pregame arousal is pressure; when stress is heavy, athletes can become charged up and feel their adrenaline start to flow. Tension and excitement over an upcoming ordeal can create an "anticipatory response," where people display a heart and respiration rate generally reserved for much later in the playing period.[6] Thus, pressure can induce a degree of pregame activation and arousal that could otherwise be attained only through strenuous exertion, enabling players to leap to an early spark start.

Sometimes coaches try to inject a dose of inspirational pressure by dedicating play to a cherished colleague. This tradition dates back to a spontaneous and moving halftime speech delivered to his players by Notre Dame's famous coach, Knute Rockne. His evocation to "win one for the Gipper" made deceased star George Gipp's memory live forever through the now oft-used metaphor. The level of performance inspired to honor someone special further highlights the moving potential of emotionally forceful pep talks and coaching.

Athletes vary, though, in their reactions to pressure. Some are "pressure players," only able to rise to their heights of excellence when much is at stake. Others never handle it well, finding adequate arousal in low degrees of pressure. For them, situations of intense stress have adverse effects on performance as they crumble and become psyched out:

> It is only myth that the World Series is a display of Spartan grandeur in which sun-hardened men face their sternest of tests with great calm and swift purpose. In fact, the World Series offers the greatest collection of manic fears and neurotic torments—the terminal jitters—this side of a psychiatrist's couch [Furlong, 1976: 28].

Thus, pressure, when applied at the wrong moment or to an extreme degree, can cause both physical and mental disruptions in performance. The adrenaline rush and corresponding tension increase can lead to "choking in the clutch." Shortness of breath, blurred vision, distorted coordination, muscle fatigue, and "death grip" (tightly knotted muscles) are common side effects. This last symptom, "co-contraction," makes the agonist and antagonist muscles contract simultaneously, reducing the body's capacity for smooth and flowing motion. Beyond physiological manifestations, psychological pressure may lead to anxiety, affecting judgment and concentration. Players may find this distracting and hypnotic, ruining strategy, effort and skill development, and even leading to serious psychosomatic ailments.[7] Outward displays of anxiety can often be misleading to teammates, opponents, and even the individual involved. Reactions to this psyched-out state vary enormously:

> Some athletes feel very tired and sleepy, yawn and even fall asleep. Some athletes joke, or act out an unconcerned and devil-may-care attitude to conceal their real anxiety. Some pretend indifference and assert great pre-contest confidence in their ultimate success. All these symptoms are physiological escape mechanisms [Lawther, 1972: 75-76].

Thus, arousal, depending on its type (pleasant/unpleasant) and level (high/low) provides the physiological power that can fuel action along a chosen path.

We see from this overall discussion that achieving a positive pregame preparation for momentum is vastly complex and important. If participants can approach an event in an upward-spiraling or "soced up" condition, with their opponents psyched out and beginning to spiral downward, they have gained a winning edge before ever starting to compete. With pregame motivation, emotions and arousal aligned into a positive, synchronized stance, the inertia of immobility begins to crumble and movement commences toward the goal. In contrast, when trying to spring from an uncertain base of confusion or fear, the effort must first be expended to overcome this negative impulse and regain the neutral point before vigorous forward motion can begin.

Early Game

One of the characteristics common to play during the early stages of a game is the *cold start*. It takes a while for people to get their bodies physically warmed up and, even more important, adjusted to the rhythm of play. For this reason, the beginning period may subjectively seem to drag on longer than the rest of the contest, where rhythmic synchrony has been achieved. The preparation stage thus continues through this early period of movement devoid of momentum. The commencement of an event or series of sporting events is also unique, because there is little previous success to build on. As one racquetball pro explained,

> the first match of a tournament's always your hardest because you don't have any momentum built up through the tournament, you don't know how you're gonna be playing, you're just cold.

Often contestants begin by *"feeling out"* (Goffman, 1959: 191-192) their adversaries, both parties initially playing conservatively. Slowly and gradually revealing their game plans, each "puts out feelers" to interpret opponents' strategies. This strategy is customary in professional football, especially during important games where much can be lost; no team wants to be the first to take a chance and expose a weakness. Oftentimes this conservative start signifies a lack of momentum on either side. Descartes' discussion of zero momentum applies very well to this sport situation (as it does to later periods of the contest), for when two antagonists of equal force vie for advantage, their efforts nullify each other and the center of mass (line of scrimmage or score) remains constant.

Structural factors framing athletic contests are also highly influential in the type of action that will develop on the playing field. One element affecting momentum opportunities is *location*: Will the event be played inside or outside, in warm or cold weather, on natural grass, artificial turf, clay, or concrete? Environmental conditions can be paramount, particularly if some contestants are more familiar with the surroundings than others. Here we come upon the elusive but ubiquitous *home court advantage*. A famous example existed in NCAA college basketball:

> It's not that UCLA can't lose in Pauley Pavillion. After all, they lose a game there every six years. . . . It [home court advantage]

> is an amalgam of local knowledge ["UCLA knows every bump in that floor"], hostility of the natives ["we get 500 seats, Arizona gets 500 seats, Las Vegas, Nevada, gets 500 seats—and UCLA gets 11,481"] and the comfort of knowing the other guy is playing your game [Murray, 1976: 1].

One factor posited to explain the higher percentage of victories at home than on the road is familiarity with the local playing turf. This extends to the relaxation gained from leading a normal social existence, eating at home, and sleeping in familiar quarters. Another theory accounting for this difference is the weariness and strain of travel, which inevitably shows more at the end of a long trip than the beginning. Late evening flights immediately following games offset the sleep schedule, leaving little time to unwind. In addition, Schwartz and Barsky (1977) have documented that importance of audience support as a major cause of markedly improved home performance. Their statistical analyses show the profoundest effects occurring for indoor sports (basketball and hockey), where crowd noise and ferver are most influential because of the confined area.

A psychological boost from the crowd can be influential in many ways. As social facilitation theory (Zajonc, 1965) suggests, it heightens emotional and psychological arousal, which facilitates performance. Reinforcement theory offers another account, calling favorable spectator reactions both a positive reward that induces further successful play,[8] and a negative reinforcer for visiting athletes. As one professional racquetball player summed it up,

> if everybody in the crowd's against you and every time you make a good shot they boo, it's really a negative reinforcer for you because you subconsciously don't want to make another shot and have them all boo. You'd rather hear them clap whether or not it's a bad shot. You want to be accepted by the crowd.

Schwartz and Barsky's conclusion is that the "integrity, vitality and self-consciousness of the home community" is the crucial factor in the home advantage; a reciprocal commitment and integration binds local areas with their representative athletes, and this unison finds expression in the momentum of the team.

MOMENTUM STARTERS

With all the components of the preparation process set in motion and the individual or team starting to strive for the desired goal, the opportunity at last exists for momentum to emerge. It can develop and gain recognition via a number of routes: in a flash of light, through a gradual process, as a recapture of something lost (the "second wind"), or as a preordained fact (carrying over from previous performance). The birth of momentum occurs through an *impetus* that thrusts performance quality to rise above the ordinary vicissitudes of play. Momentum-infused action can be launched from the total stagnation of inertia or from the frustrated motion that expends effort and covers ground but lacks luster, efficiency, and grace. This first burst or gradually achieved measure of exciting, superior play must contain enough force to overcome all the structural, behavioral, and psychological resistances to rapid, dynamic progress. Such impetus is not sufficient to sustain locomotion, but merely serves to break through the restraining barrier and inaugurate effective progress toward the goal. This is analogous to Descartes' discussion of collisions, where an active force crashed into an immobile one, pushing it onto a path of movement. Socially, this corresponds either to some competitors fiercely attacking their opponents and sending them into a downward, negative spiral, or to one team member launching others into a joint upward spiral with the force of his or her positive propulsion. Impetus thus represents the behavioral result of Newton's "impulse," an energizing force limited in existence by space and time, and to arousal theory's "impact," referring to the effect one body or force has on another.

Spark Starts

One of the greatest thrills for a sports enthusiast is to witness or experience the inception of momentum when it occurs in an instantaneous manner. A wide range of *charismatic plays* can function as catalysts, speeding up the tempo of a game and giving impetus to one side: "Some games need a spark to come alive—a fight, an embarrassment, a referee's call, or an inspiring individual effort" (Bradley, 1976: 188). A stolen base, a dunk shot, these can be "seat risers" that initiate energetic explosions: The dunk shot is "like a home run in baseball or the long bomb in football. It's worth more than two points that go up on the board because it gets the crowd and the rest of the team all excited" (Los Angeles Times, 1976a). Similarly, the actions of a *charismatic player* can spark a team into the start to momentum:

> The importance of the so-called sixth man [the first substitute] cannot be overestimated. You must have a man who can come off the bench when things are going wrong to get you untracked with a quick basket or two, a sparkling steal that will get your running game going, or so much spirit that it infects the others on the floor. . . . The kind of man I'm talking about is almost always a highly emotional individual who gets instant adrenalin flowing as soon as you call his name [Wooden, 1972: 122].

Taking a chance can jar a team into action. A play that goes against the book, something daringly unexpected, may precipitate a surge. The move need not be successful to have this effect. A play like the suicide squeeze in baseball is electric and chancy in its title alone.

Conversely, if an adversary has a good chance of scoring or winning and miscarries, the momentum may reverse by default. Should a team get runners on bases with no outs and fail to bring them home, the opponent will feel that they have achieved a victory and potentially captured the advantage.

Some coaches believe they can propagate momentum by *creating a scene* (Goffman, 1959, 210).[9] Indulgence (and encouraging players to do likewise) in yelling and berating umpires serves to arouse emotional feelings among teammates:

> There is, perhaps, an element of pleasing the crowd in some coaches' angry protestations at unfavorable or close decisions. . . . As a consequence of a protest a team may exert extra effort, being buoyed up by the defense or by a momentary exhibition of solidarity [Weiss, 1969: 170].

Engaging in fights follows the same principle (see Faulkner, 1976: 109). Many teams have rules that direct the entire bench to empty onto the playing field should a fight arise:

> Houk believed that fights woke teams up and made them play better. . . . [He] would have a team meeting and he'd say something like, "Now, don't anyone be afraid to start something. If you get into a fight we'll all be with you" [Bouton, 1970: 151].

Ironically, momentum can also be ignited by chance. An umpire's close-call decision in favor of a team can give it renewed hope and vigor. Sun, wind, or any outside factors can combine to produce the necessary spark.

Gradual Starts

If not fortunate enough to achieve the impetus toward momentum in a dramatic, instantaneous fashion, players may have to work for it slowly and agonizingly. How this transpires varies between those sports that direct competition against a single other opponent versus those where individual performance is measured against the universe of time-clock records and humanity.

In situations where players compete alone or against a broad spectrum of others (e.g., distance running, automobile racing), the intensity of focus is directed primarily inward. Here the gradual development of momentum is based solely on their own selves: energy, attitude, strategy, and timing. With a carefully controlled and engineered start it is possible to work slowly through the various stages of performance, gradually loosening up and shifting into higher gears until that desired plateau of execution is achieved. The efforts of fellow competitors, with some exceptions, are generally secondary to the inner game plan. While the struggle against the forces of resistance that affects people's ability to achieve momentum is vital (and will be discussed extensively throughout this work), let us turn our attention temporarily to the actively antagonistic relationship between players, and their attempts to wrest momentum from each other as well as from their inner selves (which also overlaps considerably with the less directly combative model).

Most games follow the dominant two-sided form that yields a winner and a loser. Here, the adversary's performance has a direct and immediate effect on one's own, as it is unusual for both parties to achieve momentum simultaneously. In the overwhelming majority of cases, Leibniz and Newton's contention that for every action (positive momentum) there exists an equal and opposite reaction (negative momentum) is accurate. But as we have already seen, humans do not always live by the laws governing inanimate objects, and sometimes *dual momentum* develops. We can witness this rare phenomenon in a basketball game, for example, where both sides get "hot" and blaze with unfailing offensive capacity:

> It would surround not only me and the other Celtics but also the players on the other team, and even the referees. To me, the key was that *both* teams had to be playing at their peaks, and they had to be competitive. The Celtics could not do it alone [Russell and Branch, 1979: 155].

Usually, however, any indication of weakness or strength by an opponent will be reflected inversely in the other's ability to develop momentum. Athletes observe the flow of the game, watching for indications that their force is beginning to succeed over the antagonist's. The brief but small advantages (ebb and flow) that can be gained from a couple of plays are usually not considered significant until they begin to form into a pattern.

But once the recognizable model of escalation occurs and is noted by either competitor, they have achieved through a gradual process the first step to superlative performance: the impetus.

Several factors can be influential in helping players develop an edge over each other. During the game, as well as before, the strategy of psyching out the opponent to gain an advantage is noteworthy.[10] Some athletes work the soft approach, trying to throw their adversaries off balance by being overly solicitous and evoking guilt feelings. Most rely on hard-line provocation, throwing verbal barbs, cold shoulders, or working complex con games.[11] In turn, athletes try to counteract these strategies through Zen-like methods of total concentration and relaxation (see Herrigel, 1953). Athletes often feel that their performance develops in direct proportion to their ability to focus exclusively on the playing terrain or equipment, screening out inner thoughts and other outside distractions. Concentration is thus a crucial contributor to the gradual start of power play.

Factors stemming from outside players can further enhance the gradual start of momentum. Territoriality[12] is a significant external force, as certain portions of a playing field have more crucial meaning to participants and thereby evoke the energy necessary to defend them. This is particularly applicable to football: Ground near the end zone is more significant than that in the middle of the field. Defensive goal-line stands illustrate this, where a team may be pushed back nearly to its end zone during a drive, yet hold off repeated scoring attempts from the one-yard line.

Just as teams get stingy when territory is running low,they may react when *time* starts closing in. Every sport and contest has its own subjective time dynamics (see Weiss, 1969: 163, 178; Lyman and Scott, 1970: 189-212), where the hands of the clock seem to race or stand still. Some games do not pick up or get interesting until the end:

> Good teams have a tendency to be complacent. It is as if we tempted fate, sure of our ability to rescue any situation before

disaster. The realization that a loss was imminent jarred us to action [Bradley, 1976: 188].

Here, "time panic" suddenly set in and caused the team to achieve that necessary impetus, that super-level of play.

On occasions, the thrust to momentum (like the home court advantage) can come from the audience. With cheerleaders screaming, organ and trumpet sounding "charge," or the fans clapping rhythmically and yelling "de-fense, de-fense," the players are inspired to greater heights. The relationship between these different types of participants, watcher and watched, can be keen: "The Bird's relationship with the crowd is a two-way street. 'They get me up,' he says, 'I can hear all of them. It gets the adrenalin flowing even more.' " (Los Angeles Times, 1976b). Interaction between players and spectators, therefore, does not fall outside the domain of the game. Fan promotion, or lack of it, can directly affect athletes' performances.

Regenerating Energy: The Second Wind

Occasionally, after playing for a while and battling frustratedly against the elements, an athlete will feel winded and "out of steam." Legs and arms get weak, seem hollow, and the whole body begins to feel exhausted physically and mentally. Etiologically, this is probably a combination of physiological exertion, psychological strain, and falling into an unrecognized performance rut. In extreme cases the associated sensations can seem unbearable. One bicycle racer explained, "You get to the point where your body's just killing you—the pain, pain. You can't catch your breath, the sweat is blinding your eyes and your muscles are aching to the point of collapse." Then suddenly a flood of energy appears, relieving the pain and revitalizing the body's supply of power. All at once the fatigue disappears, the feeling of despair is alleviated, and movement proceeds effortlessly. This phenomenon, known to many as the *second wind*, is a familiar process that has barely been investigated. From the halting depths of torpidity and exertion, people nearly instantaneously shift into high gear, bypassing intermediary levels.

Here, the pause in pace occasioned by the slight let-up during those feelings of exhaustion seems to release a momentum of explosive intensity. The rapid ascension thus involves a felt decrease in energy output, with less effort needed to sustain greater accomplishment. A marathon runner described his experience: "It feels as if you were running up an incline for about three miles and then all of a sudden the road levels out or even starts going downhill. . . . I had a second wind the other day that came orgasmically, where I literally shifted into overdrive and felt suddenly better and more relaxed."

Many athletes describe this as a return to the original energy level of commencement, except that by the time this occurs they are completely warmed up and performing with fluidity. Further, they repeatedly speak of a threshold point, wherein once a portion of the difficult task is achieved the remainder becomes easy.

For some, this second wind is a unique breakthrough that can never be repeated during the course of an activity. The renewed vigor gained can eventually erode, but still one is never as weary as just before it "kicks in." Others report experiencing third and fourth winds (ad infinitum), but say that it is harder to perceive them because the change is not as dramatic, the tuning is finer. One racquetball player suggested that due to the radical stop-and-go pace of his game he was consistently experiencing multiple "miniwinds" throughout each contest.

Players further differ in their conception of how this regeneration of energy and capacity can be achieved. One group regards it as an uncontrollable force that erupts essentially without warning. As expressed by one marathoner, they believe that in the throes of exhaustion, "you gotta keep going. The first wind, don't bother about what other people around you are racing, just keep loose in your heart and the second wind's gonna get there sooner or later."

Others approach the subject with a greater degree of initiative, maintaining that by remaining sensitive to the body's condition one can know the most opportune time to call upon inner reserves. Rather than passively waiting for a second wind, they cultivate the ability to draw it out at will. One tennis player outlined his beliefs:

> When competing seriously, physical endurance becomes a real property. It's an absolute necessity that a competent player be able to "reach down" and get that second wind, that regeneration of physical energy that you've lost due to fatigue, and to pick up again at a winning pace. This takes a certain amount of willpower and practice. In fact, in preparing for a tournament we practice to generate a fatigued feeling so we *can* reach down after we can't go anymore, and then we practice some more.

An altogether different perspective on the second wind entails its function as a change and relaxation of pace. Proponents of this attitude explain that the beginning of play, constituting the first wind, is usually characterized by an overtense condition. This initial nervous, explosive energy eventually burns off, leaving the player exhausted and leg weary. Suddenly this tiredness too disappears, succeeded by a refreshment and revitalization, the body no longer hampered by being wound up in knots. Tension is replaced with a calm, relaxed feeling, characterized by fluidity and ease of movement. This view of regenerating momentum is more aptly called a *second pace*, as its recapture of energy is secondary to achieving the loosened, restful tempo and gait characteristic of "placid" momentum.

Several physiological explanations have been proposed to account for the second wind phenomenon, but no single hypothesis has emerged as dominantly accepted. One theory holds that during strenuous exercise the body's core or internal temperature rises in response to exertion. Once the level of heat stabilizes throughout the entire system, the second wind is achieved. A second viewpoint focuses on oxygen content in the bloodstream and tissues, suggesting that the second wind represents a steady state where inhalation of oxygen is finally sufficient to feed the body's needs. Last, some scientists look at the way exercise causes catecholamines, adrenaline, and noradrenaline to burn off, positing that when the adrenaline and blood glucose levels reach a comfortable medium the second wind appears.[13]

These physiological theories describe the changing internal biochemistry that marks the onset of the second wind. But their accounts are ultimately ex post facto and cannot explain why this state can serve as an impetus and springboard to the qualitatively different level and type of performance that characterizes momentum. Perhaps the answer lies at least partly in the perceptual domain, the *sense* of second wind arising as concentration is lifted from some secondary concern and is redirected toward expending effort on the activity immediately at hand. Then, for a brief period, the full depths of energy resources are applied and an easier, more successful performance flow results.

ESTABLISHING MOMENTUM

An individual or team may have all the aforementioned elements—psych, readiness, a lucky break, and a charismatic display—but if they are unable to back up this auspicious start with a sustaining surge, it will never attain full momentum. As noted in Chapter 2, the impetus that characterizes the initial thrust is fleeting, lasting for an insignificant duration. Combatants who want to attain momentum and win must be able to act on that evanescent power with carry-through force, transforming it into a drive of enduring time and achievement.

> Every so often a Celtic game would heat up so that it became more than a physical or even mental game, and would be magical. . . . When it happened I could feel my play rise to a new level. It came rarely, and would last anywhere from five minutes to a whole quarter. Three or four plays were not enough to get it going [Russell and Branch, 1979: 155].

In many cases the impulse swiftly subsides, but without adequate temporal persistence it cannot be considered momentum; it resembles the engine spark that fails to evoke ignition. A team that creates or is presented with momentary advantages but neglects to seize and utilize them has experienced only limited thrust and failed to generate inner propulsion. Leibniz's sociologically converted primitive and derivative forces can be seen to join here. Clearly, the start to momentum embodied in the impetus constitutes the former kind of force. But the latter, springing from the efforts and results of that initial start, is recognizable in this carry-through phase of momentum creation. Therefore, as an individual or team begins to build a positive flow, the very elements that fostered it continue to operate and press for more progress. Simultaneously, the effects the initial impetus has had on the surrounding environment will return to feed back into the fledgling motion, further reinforcing it. Once developing momentum is perceived, its creator(s) may feel more positive, confident, and effervescent. Conversely, if an adversary senses the opposition getting "revved," an element of doubt and despair can arise. Inner deterioration may be further accompanied by a faulting performance. Hence the nascent positive momentum for one party may signify inchoate negative momentum for another; and once a drive is established, the competition's downward spiraling execution generally intensifies too, contributing more thrust to the positive ascension. One racquetball player analyzed this relationship:

> When the guy I'm playing against starts getting a string of "hot" shots going, it's really tough on me because when you've got it, you've got it; he starts making these off the wall shots no one in their right mind would even try and then I can't even use my regular defense against him. And because I want the serve back so badly I'll take the poorer percentage shots to stop him and my offense falls apart too, so he thrives on that.

Physiological preparation can be seen as critical to crystallizing a burgeoning momentum because the ensuring, excited state may temporarily abort any rational playing strategy that may have been formulated. Here, the long, grueling practice hours are rewarded as ingrained muscle pathways take over automatically. Although skills are adaptable and not completely routinized, our reflexes often react by habit to familiar cues, particularly in situations where there is little time to think (Lawther, 1972: 19). This differentiates between the momentum-developing capability of beginners and that of experienced players: The latter group can rely on their bodies' *learned responses* to function successfully during critical periods, while novices who lack competently established motor memory cannot.

Several factors intrinsic to play can contribute to establishing momentum. The ability to *capitalize on other players' mistakes* is crucial. Good play is more effective at certain times than at others; by following up opponents' errors with successful maneuvers, players can generate added velocity and intensity. This is because their adversaries may be depressed from having made mistakes, and hitting them hard causes a multiplier effect, intensifying the downward spiral. For example, when a basketball is stolen, if points are not scored players often feel that the steal has done little good. Further, when a baseball fielder makes an error and allows a runner on base, if the team at bat fails to drive in the run, not only have they squandered an opportunity, but they have emotionally demoralized themselves.

> A team that can sense, or diagnose, the opposition's letdowns and exploit them quickly is well on its way to victory. Some teams explicitly incorporate such diagnosis into their strategy. When their opponents are playing at their peak they try to hold them to a standoff. They wait for a sign of weakness, then turn up the pressure. They "play for the breaks," capitalize on weakness, exploit opportunities [Novak, 1976: 140].

In contrast, when competitors are presented with a timely situation but are unable to capitalize on it, the originally erring players are given new life and their own impetus to momentum. One tennis player explained why this occurs: "When I hit a couple of bad shots and my opponent doesn't take advantage of it—they just drill them into the ground—I say, 'Hey, I've got a second chance,' and I start playing a little better."

Coming through in the clutch is one of the most important elements in establishing momentum. Here a sense of timing is the key, as success escapes many potentially excellent teams whose hits and advances are plentiful, but never put together in the right combination. The "big play" remains elusive.

Absolute control of momentum requires a *"Killer instinct,"* that inner drive to destroy an opponent when he or she is down rather than letting up and softening.

> Russell's commitment to the game was different from other players, who treated basketball as a job and had difficulty developing the killer instinct. For Russell there seemed to be no separation between basketball success/failure and the rest of life [Bradley, 1976: 184].

Similarly, in boxing, the occasional jab followed by dancing and crowd-pleasing antics is not nearly as brutally effective as a serious attack to the "jugular vein," where pugilists follow successful punches with a continual barrage, though their own energy is sapped.

MOMENTUM REALIZED

Once these requisites have been fulfilled, the peak period of movement, exhilaration, and progress can occur, and players truly experience the feeling of momentum. Finally, the individual or team is "in the groove," the "vibes" are right, and everyone moves fluidly. All at once players cannot miss the strike zone, or there is a "magic rainbow" between their fingers and the basketball hoop.

> Suddenly we "caught fire." Everything we shot went in and our defense held Milwaukee scoreless for five minutes. We won by three points, accomplishing what came to be known as a

"believer feat." Those who saw it believed in our invincibility. I even think we did [Bradley, 1976: 92].

Sometimes momentum is electricity incarnate, people endowed with it spinning effortlessly yet sustaining a nearly perfect flow that feels mystically sparkling and crazy. Or the sensation may be more like floating, as if all actions were conducted in slow motion, everything linking gracefully together. A reporter, interviewing tennis star Chris Evert after she won the U.S. Open, quotes her as "feeling 'spacey.' I felt like any ball I hit would be a winner." The reporter writes that Miss Evert "found that lovely feeling of total contentedness and played as if she were in a sweet dream" (Cohen, 1977: 3).

These descriptions highlight the strong elements of *rhythm, pace,* and *tempo* associated with sport. Play is smooth and effortless, participants gliding over the field, accomplishing extraordinary feats. Vanished are the unalterably rough and choppy movements continuously broken by stumbling blocks of awkwardness. When "in the zone," one has control over breathing and execution of action, slowing down to a desired regularity or dancing over the court, streaming excitedly with great speed.

A sensation of *confidence* prevails, leading to rhythmic pulsation and an inner, heady glow. People develop faith in their natural ability to excel, becoming completely infused with a positive optimism that breeds further success. One football player exulted, "It changes your whole self-image if you're with a group of guys that are good; everybody knows they're good, and you're coming on the field; you're a Miami Dolphin."

Numerous athletes also remark that their *perception* becomes altered during momentum encounters. They experience changes in all their senses which make tasks more clearly defined and easier to execute. Pitcher Bob Feller, a member of baseball's Hall of Fame, admits that when flirting with a no-hitter, "the ball feels the size of a pea" (Cohen, 1977: 3). A world-class international fencer explains, "Once I get my momentum in a match I get more acutely aware of distance, the tip of my weapon, the moves my opponent's going to use, all the things that are important in fencing."

Further, the actual *style of play* is affected. Whether through conscious strategy or by purely instinctual reaction, athletes report an altered tenor to their actions. Movements that were previously sluggish become crisp, running strides become relaxed and loping, all-around execution approaches perfection. Realizing this, players enlarge their repertoire of moves, taking chances on difficult acts that they would ordinarily consider too risky or "bad-percentage." During momentum, even the off-hand or accidental movement that would normally result in a gaffe usually finds its way to success.

Although the flow of momentum, once it has been attained, resembles a rough plateau complicated by occasional irregularities and shifts of the intensity level, a peak within this already elevated period is conceivable. Such an ultimate climax takes the form of a "magic moment," that special instant when players' inner forces and the surrounding climate of inter-personal and structural factors synchronize to produce a perfect play that is desperately needed and symbolically significant. The height of charismatic play, this immortalizing achievement may be the result of a lifetime's worth of momentum build-up, yielding a fulfilling and exhilarating experience. Such a feeling overcame Bobby Thompson when he hit his famous "shot heard 'round the world" to come from behind and clinch the 1951 National League pennant for the New York Giants.

Yet for a preponderant majority of positive momentum cases, an inverse counterpart, *negative momentum*, can be found. As has been previously discussed, the impetus offered and sustained by one athletic party often draws its sustenance and strength from the downfall of an opponent. Yet this is not the only form a competitive situation can take. In addition to encounters where a high-energy, dynamic quality exists on both sides, there can be situations where that quality is absent from both contenders. Dull contests occur when the antagonists are equally lackluster and seem to vie for the greater ineptitude.

When "out of synch" in this manner, a team feels like it has received the "kiss of death":

> Everything we do goes wrong. It is as if no one wants to touch the ball, much less shoot it. No one will take the offensive responsibility. When one of us finally asserts himself, it is outside the flow of the team and leads to forced shots. . . . Our defense plays listlessly. . . . Frustration shows on our faces [Bradley, 1976: 185-186].

In sports not characterized by the single, highly visible opponent, negative momentum can arise purely through the internal actions of the individual or squad. Often this takes the reverse, mirror image of its positive sibling in developing: A single, disastrous event can destroy confidence and morale, causing the players to plummet into a downward spiral that feeds off its very failure.

Players report a strong feeling of helplessness associated with this condition, as if trapped into the decline and unable to break out of it. Whatever they do brings horrible results. This collapse of physical competence brings what one racquetball player described as a stream of mental anguish and reexamination of self: "When even the routine or automatic shots just aren't working, you begin to develop a question mark in your own mind about your game and your game skills."

A completely pessimistic attitude then takes over, and people begin to expect to lose. Players demoralized like this often fall back upon a routine and lifeless style of play, merely "going through the motions." In team events, they may try to cover only their own position, stripped of the aggressiveness which characterizes forward momentum. Individuals, too, fall into a defensive posture that alters their basic game plan. When things start going wrong nobody is willing to take chances, choosing instead the safe route that usually guarantees a loss. Randy Rasmussen, offensive tackle for the New York Jets, calls this "the difference between making an ordinary play and a superior play. . . . You're looking for a way out of the responsibility. You're making excuses" (Jacobsen, 1978: B2).

When caught in the grip of negative momentum there is always somebody else to blame. Teammates turn on each other, individual athletes on their supporting personnel and everybody on the referees. Players call this "losers' talk" and know it for a part of the "deterioration syndrome."

MOMENTUM BREAKERS

We have observed how momentum erupts and is sustained, but most often it sputters and perishes. Extrapolation from principles of physics suggests that the termination of such a force is inevitable, since human beings operate within a real world filled with resistance pressures like gravity, fatigue, and adversity. The artificial boundaries in sport, however, make it theoretically possible for a momentum surge to continue without waning. An individual or team can forge ahead at crest performance without fading throughout a single contest or season. Further, players' peaking can continue until their careers in sport are finished by retirement or ultimately death. Yet aside from these extraordinary exceptions, the excitement, intensity, and superior execution associated with momentum will ultimately expire.

> The intensity of football is so high that no team can maintain its highest levels indefinitely. A reversal of fortunes, the weariness of a key player, a sudden spasm of self-doubt, a brilliant play by the opposition against one's own best effort—all these can momentarily take the edge off one's own certainty, confuse one's instincts. Sheer steady talent can hold off the deluge. But the difference between acting at one's peak and becoming cautious is a very fine one [Novak, 1976: 140].

Internal Momentum Breakers

Psychologists offer a variety of suggestions illuminating the nature of interruptions in momentum that stem from within.

Arousal level can decrease as the result of a sustaining stimulus wearing off or being removed (drive theory). This occurs, for example, when a formidable foe who inspires maximum output in adversaries by his or her presence alone is withdrawn from a game either temporarily or through defeat. Also, as Fiske and Maddi (1961) posit, the energizing influence of an initial provocation may begin to abate as its "relative novelty" erodes through acclimation. Another explanation is that inner drive simply cannot be sustained for long periods, since the individual or team tires physically and mentally. This "running out of gas" is manifested in a natural "letdown," where top-level performance gives way to emotional exhaustion and reduced efficiency (Lawther, 1972: 78). For example, teams that expend themselves in catching up from behind may be especially unable to maintain their momentum beyond the break-even point, failing in their quest for victory.

Psychological freezing is not uncommon either, as the athlete who is doing well may experience an uncontrollable and often unrecognized fear of success. One amateur racquetball player expressed the problem this way:

> I don't know what's the matter with me, but I seem to specialize in giving my opponents come-from-behind victories. Every time I get ahead by 13 to 2 or so, something happens and I just let up in my game. I lose all the momentum I had and with it the match.

A different type of freezing that may generate similar outcomes involves the mental stop-action of *stepping back to assess the situation*. In the midst of play people often do this, evaluating everyone's performance and their progress in the game. The results can be disastrous, because the natural rhythmic flow is shattered and cannot easily be regained. One professional racquetball player describes how this happened to her:

> I was really moving well; my energy was so compact and I was using it when I should. Then I stepped back, looked at where I

> was, and I thought, "this girl is just levels above myself—I can't believe I'm beating her 9 to 2." I kind of lost my confidence in myself then, or else I exceeded what I wanted to do in the game. I had just hoped to give her a good game and I got my goal. So I just put the ball in play instead of going for those last 2 points; I changed my whole style of play and fell apart.

This example highlights another potential momentum breaker generated by the individual: posing *low levels of aspiration.* In establishing a modest desired achievement, athletes may save their egos from being deflated, but they can also preclude the possibility of finer play and grander success. An automatic effort shutoff can be unconsciously implanted, triggered when the predetermined aim is accomplished.

A team that is in the lead and playing well may purposefully or inadvertently *sidetrack* or *switchtrack* (Lyman and Scott, 1970: 199), changing the style or rhythm of play. Participants may modify their game when competing against friends, trying to win by the lowest possible margin—as with jockeys (Scott, 1968) and pool hustlers (Polsky, 1967)—or seeking to spare the opponent embarrassment. Moreover, in timed events, a team will often slow the pace to "run down the clock." College basketball is particularly known for a variety of sidetracking techniques employed to preserve a lead in the closing minutes by "milking the clock" and "freezing the ball." Football units employ a related strategy, running the ball on every play instead of mixing in passes, so as not to stop the clock. The drawback, however, is that a group may lose its competitive edge as it deviates from the successful game plan and adopts a new style. Should the competitors seize this chance to initiate their own momentum, the leaders may be bypassed in the closing minutes or seconds.

External Momentum Breakers

Outside the realm of individual players, a number of factors stand as potential hazards to established momentum. Two chief nemeses are *interruption* and *intrusion* (Lyman and Scott, 1970:

147). Anything that disturbs the rhythm and tempo of a game can reverse the pace and advantage. Inclement weather delays are obvious momentum breakers, resulting in inactivity and muscle-tightening. A long wait stifles almost any rally and contributes to a team's demise. Human elements can provide equally distressing intrusions in the form of uprisings among fans (e.g., garbage-throwing) that temporarily halt play. By the time things quiet down, someone is likely to have "gone cold."

This phenomenon resembles one aspect of the role of *time-outs*: the reduction of tension and arousal. In contrast to casual social interaction, where high intensity often feels awkward, sporting situations thrive on an increased energy state. Athletes feed off this atmosphere, seeking to ascend to higher plateaus. Cognizant of this, a team will try to "flood out" an opposing team that is beginning to attain a higher level of energy (Goffman, 1961: 55) by calling a time-out.[14] This allows the team to regroup strategically while disrupting the successful play of the opponent. One racquetball player described how he did this:

> When I feel like my opponent is getting hot, I immediately call a time-out, because a lot of people score and hurry back to the line to serve again—they want to keep what they have going. So I'll take as much time as I can to defray their momentum. I'll just do little things to slight them, like take my full 10 seconds, call a time-out and get a towel and wipe up the floor, even if there's no wet spot. This stops them cold.

Hence, a time-out can furnish someone the opportunity to change the pace of a game and take control over the vital elements of timing.

Ironically, time-outs can also serve the opposite function, increasing the tension instead of breaking it. Commonly in football, a halt is called by the defensive team just prior to a field goal attempt. The kicker, then, is forced to ponder the impending kick to the extent that he may tense up and miss it.

Unusual incidents (Goffman, 1959: 212; Lyman and Scott, 1970: 148) or unwanted occurrences can lead to breaks in momentum. Embarrassments or humiliations may fluster players and teams into losing their cool. Olympic play contains a plethora of such examples: When divers or gymnasts make a gaffe in front of judges and international television, they may never recover their confidence and poise. An error in baseball may be so keenly felt that the whole team momentarily falls apart. A single incident may destroy in an instant what it took days, months, or even years to build.

Personal problems, difficult to leave off the field, can intrude to break the spiral of momentum. External worries can wreck anyone's game:

> "It was a bitch to play baseball with all the worries about bill collectors. I thought any day one of them would run on the field and serve me in front of twenty thousand people. I'd go up to bat, the pitcher would release the ball, and I'd see a bill flying up to the plate" (Pepitone, 1975: 140).

Even if problems in one's life are escaped, a plethora of other kinds of sports-related troubles can come to mind at any time and offset a performance. Hassles with management, coaches, or other players, once relatively rare, have now become an integral part of the professional sports scene and a deleterious influence on quality play.

External to the performance of players is the disaster of *prop failure* (Lyman and Scott, 1970: 147). Here, a nonhuman component of the sport may temporarily falter or break completely, leaving the participants helpless. Baseball players are particularly superstitious about such events, attaching magical significance to their clothes and tools (Gmelch, 1972: 134; Bouton, 1970). If, during a hitting streak, a player's lucky bat breaks, he may despair and flounder, convinced that the hits were a property of the bat, not him.

Loss of a key player (or coach) due to injury or penalties can also abort a drive in midstream. Aside from the obvious absence of this player's talent, fellow athletes can become emotionally disspirited by such a departure and their group balance be adversely affected (soced out). Ejection by penalty occurs frequently in most established professional sports, but the possibility of injury prevails in any game. In either case, an offensive drive under way may suffer severe hardship.

Even with all team members present and able, *lack of teamwork* can crush momentum. Group sports depend on the fluid and equitable interworking of individuals striving for the benefit of the whole rather than "hotdogging" (showing off) for selfish glory. A professional basketball player voices his feelings on this issue:

> When you have momentum you have to play together. On my team I'm the "playmaker," the one who directs the team on the court. I can't hold the ball when I should be passing it to a good shooter. Nothing breaks momentum more than one guy holding onto the ball and shooting a lot himself instead of playing a team game.

Last, *audience effects* can be substantial in contributing to the destruction of momentum. As noted, when playing on foreign turf athletes often feel intimidated by the crowd. Their inner urges for audience acceptance vie with the conscious, rational desire to succeed, occasionally rattling them enough that they lose their graceful synchrony. Spectators can be distracting, too, even if they have the best intentions of supporting and cheering for their team. Varying with the sport, players frequently find that fans' irritating vocalizations (or worse) either break their concentration or overarouse them (Zajonc, 1965), leaving the momentum so assiduously undertaken to slip through their fingers and shatter.

The realization that momentum is breaking or broken can be soberingly depressing. One loses not only the benefit of that extra thrust and velocity, but the special feeling of being in an unusual and heightened state, one that is completely absorbing and satisfying. When this passes sooner than desired, various feelings are evoked, ranging from rage to emptiness. When the smoothness associated with momentum begins to lapse, the athlete is left hanging on to whatever shreds of intensity and suppleness can be mustered ("coasting"). Further, the conscious recognition of descent to a normal, mundane pace and tempo speeds momentum's death through the disappearance of confidence and the lost sense of magical invulnerability and omnipotence. Physically, players begin to experience again all the aches and pains that were forgotten once momentum began. The most poignant impression of privation is carried on an emotional level, as the multitude of elements that have been so carefully constructed come tumbling down. The result is despondency, hopelessness, and despair.

SEASONAL MOMENTUM

Beyond the microsetting of the everyday contest—where particularistic features of play can cause turnabout and jumps of momentum—is the long, arduous season. Athletes, especially professionals, must gear themselves for this temporal frame, becoming additionally sensitized to emotional and performance highs and lows that endure over the course of time. Socially defined *streaks* and *slumps*, consecutive strings of victories or defeats, are no longer team manifestations of the momentum process. Here, the spiral built up during the game is sustained over the interim period and released again in the subsequent games. Often players fail to understand the physical, psychological, and collective constructive mechanisms that aid their ability to hold on to momentum, attributing this to mysterious powers:

> In hopes of maintaining a batting streak, I once ate fried chicken every day at 4:00 p.m., kept my eyes closed during the national anthem and changed sweat shirts at the end of the fourth inning each night for seven consecutive nights until the streak ended [Gmelch, 1972: 131].

While talent is unquestionably instrumental in forging streaks and slumps, there are other dynamic factors that contribute as well. Inner synchronization of the key subcomponents that focus attitude, concentration, and coordination into the necessary alignment, combined with the social acknowledgement of momentum's presence, is what makes the difference between struggling with play and performing at peak potential. Sometimes this spiral alignment and perception can be contained in the euphoric feeling generated by great play. As one professional football player expressed it,

> I don't care if I win or lose but it's just so nice to win; it's such a pleasant feeling. You carry it with you the whole week, sometimes longer than that for exceptional games. So I'd say you can keep momentum for as long as you hold on to that feeling.

Teams able to create this feeling often do so because of their cohesion, drawing upon players' inner reflectiveness and interpersonal communication to enhance their sensitivity to the fragilely submerged momentum.

After a while the temporary sustaining of momentum's sensations that aids the elongation of performative streaks can be supplemented by the formation of a collectively shared sense of team confidence. This more enduring, positive self-conception builds up during periods of momentum play but stays with participants long after the game's termination. Through mutual reinforcement that focuses on successful experiences, team members come to believe they are capable of high-quality performance and even begin to expect momentum. Then, as they approach the field of play they can use this vision of their own proficiency to prevent resistance power from accumulating and launch competition with a preinstilled edge on momentum. Hence, the Dallas Cowboys' head coach Tom Landry concludes that momentum is a short-term phenomenon whose long-term product is confidence (Jacobsen, 1978: B2).

In extremely rare instances a team can exhibit such a strong collective confidence and stabilized internal synchronization that it achieves multiyear momentum. It is here that the zenith of team play can be found, lodged in a tradition of unsurpassed excellence: the dynasty. When a baseball player donned the

New York Yankee pinstripes in the 1950s and early 1960s, a magical feeling prevailed (see Golenbock, 1975). Dynastic teams can motivate performers to rise from the depths of obscurity to the pinnacle of greatness. Such a dynasty has flourished in basketball:

> On top of all other things the Boston Celtics have going for them there exists a highly emotional quality, a mystique that possesses the hearts and drives every man in kelly green and white to the utmost. They refer to it reverently as Celtic Pride [Greer, 1977].

The tradition of self-sacrifice thrives in these situations, every player, year after year, giving his or her utmost. Once the original momentum is established, various factors combine to keep it alive, transcending the talents of any one individual or seasonal combination of individuals. The emotional spur of a dynastic heritage enshrouds added team members, often eliciting from them a higher level of play than had previously been thought to exist. Thus, athletes may experience a drastic rise in performance after moving to a team with a firmly ensconced momentum.

Still, the confidence and spirit that keeps a twenty-year momentum like this alive eventually crumbles. For both the Celtics and Yankees the end came abruptly, the latter club slipping from first to sixth in a single season. This trend further underscores the role of momentum in buoying the performance of a team whose talent has eroded (through trades, aging, or retirement) beyond the period of rational accountability. Then, when the squad suddenly realizes that the magic is gone, that they too can lose, the protracted momentum bursts like a bubble.

Thus, we have witnessed the range of momentum in sport from its initial glimmer to nearly a career lifespan, influenced by physical, personal, and relational factors. Its inchoation can be charismatically dazzling or slowly but steadfastedly pursued; likewise its expiration. But while momentum endures, it conveys the gift of flawless grace, totally involved concentration, and superlative performance.

SOCIAL RELATIONS AND MOMENTUM

Permeating all sport is a social framework surrounding players' experiences and athletic endeavors. From the greater structural backdrop to the most immediate situational setting, the social reality of others helps to shape proclivities toward momentum and perceptions about it.

Social Structure

Within many sports the clearest forms of social structures are provided by the leagues, teams, and interpersonal networks that compete against each other. For individual sports, especially on the serious amateur level, these "teams" may be informal, but they are there nonetheless, in the form of family, coaching and support personnel, and athletic colleagues. Here, the models of acceptable behavior are worked out, passed along, and sanctioned. Societal attitudes favoring highly competitive interaction, encouraging discreet ruthlessness, and condoning the ideal that winning is everything are translated into reality through situational example. Even the structure of competitive play conveys the stark essence of limited good: Only one entrant can emerge victorious. The greater social structure thus sets the tone and format under which momentum will arise—where its presence is eagerly anticipated, even studiously demanded.

Social Organization

Those who coach or direct teams try to orchestrate the social organization of teams to create a climate favorable to momentum. Group solidarity and integration are vital to creating a sense of *cohesion* among club personnel that is rooted in their commonly shared joys, sorrows, experiences, and hopes. When all players have contributed to a "soced up" teamwork, satisfaction results from the combination of communication, synchronization, and mutual positive feedback. As one professional basketball player explained,

> it's important for a team to hang together, both when you're winning and when you're losing. Everything is the *team*—the

> whole unit. In order to have momentum you have to really feel and play together.

Thus, the cement that binds a team together can greatly determine the quality of play. Some refer to these abstract bonds forged by social organization and interaction as *"chemistry"*—that intangible feeling transcending the ability of each performer, which sets the tone for the group's working rapport. The nature of these relationships is critical to transforming a clutter of discrete individuals into a fluid, synchronized whole, and is therefore instrumental in evoking or precluding momentum.

Mead (1934: 152) considered the ideal sport to be highly cohesive, composed of people continuously internalizing all other players' roles. Here, the distinction between self and other is minimal, leading to the most successful interaction. Bradley (1976: 60-61) describes his sport as one that holds great potential for this conception:

> I beliive that basketball, when a certain level of unselfish team play is realized, can serve as a kind of metaphor for ultimate cooperation. It is a sport where success, as symbolized by the championship, requires that the dictates of community prevail over selfish personal impulses.

Thus, a group instilled with community spirit may aspire to greater heights than one founded on personal glory. For example, Olympic participants may find themselves infused with altruistic feelings, a sense that they are "carrying the flag."

Some sports seem to foster cooperative *modes of interaction* more than others. The structure of games can be seen as a partial determinant of cohesion, teamwork, and momentum. Pearman (1976) has delineated two types of sport: *cumulative*, in which individuals are pitted against each other and their scores totaled at the end (as in golf and bowling), and *simultaneous*, in which all players work together as a unit against another group (as in baseball and football). Because the resistance pressure facing a group of athletes is greater than it is for individual athletes, we can see how participants in cumulative sports might find it easier both to gain and to lose momentum, while simultaneous-sports participants would require more impetus to get themselves moving, but be able to sustain that attitude, quality, and momentum more easily. Yet, even within the simultaneous sports we see variations in the degree and type of interactional solidarity: Games requiring homogeneous skills (e.g., *all* members dribble, shoot, and guard) are characterized by mechanical cooperation, as contrasted with more heterogeneous recreations (*some* pitch, play infield, play outfield, and each hits separately), where organic cooperation prevails. Here, those sports with mechanical cooperation are more prone to momentum because of their greater cohesion and the similarity of their playing experience, making it easier for teammates to take each other's perspective and ignite a surge of rising quality play.[15] Hence, not only is the onset of momentum facilitated, but so is its spread.

The process of *social contagion*, so vital to transforming an initial impetus into established momentum, again hinges greatly on social relations. Stabilizing a shooting excitement and ability involves all players in becoming infused with the greater intensity. Whether the thrust to excel comes from opposing players, external forces, or a member of the group, it must spread throughout the team so that each individual is equally enthused:

> A team gains intensity and confidence from each success on the part of one member—one man's courage inspires the others. If some are playing well, but not with zest, the others tend to shepherd their own resources. A team depends on equal intensity on the part of all. If some slack off, the efforts of the others are canceled out. If all apply equal pressure, a bond of loyalty hardens the resolve of each: *I* will not be the one to let the others down. Each inspires the others to heights they otherwise would never climb [Novak, 1976: 139-140].

Contagion may be facilitated by the special feeling of team membership generated in select clubs. Players form an identification with something greater than themselves and can more easily find the motivation to train, concentrate, and exert their utmost efforts when the success or failure of the whole company is at stake.

In veteran teams, a system of sensitivity and intercommunication becomes intrinsic to their structure and routine functioning. Members experience solidarity and rely on each other to perform certain tasks. Thus, an atmosphere conducive to contagion already exists at the start of each contest—one wherein there is heightened responsiveness to cues provided by others (Turner and Killian, 1972). With this backdrop of intense physical and mental proximity, imitation and contagion can easily transpire. Excitement, anticipation, and confidence are generated at one point and passed infectiously from station to station, building and intensifying along the way. One success, especially when located in a key place, affects everybody. A recent example from professional basketball illustrates this theme. Midway through a game, Kareem Abdul-Jabbar, Los Angeles's towering center, soared through the air and slammed home a powerful "skydunk":

> "That kind of dunk gives our team an emotional lift," coach Jerry West said. "You can see the whole team rise. Kareem is our quiet leader, no question. This bunch looks to him."
>
> "When he goes up that high and throws it down," Ford said, "geez it excited me . . . and I was on the bench. It got me out of my seat for the first time that quarter." . . . "It gets you jacked up," said Lou Hudson, who scored 18 points. "That shot may even carry us over to tomorrow" [Green, 1977].

Collective Attitudes

A team's organization, interaction, cohesion, and potential for contagion can thus have marked effects on performance (the ultimate measure of momentum). These qualities can generate good or poor morale and lead one to be more "soced up" than another, influencing the way players approach each new game. Even before the contest commences, athletes possess a *generalized belief* about their ability, which influences their play and their chances of developing momentum. Shared attitudes, especially those involving a squad's optimism, confidence, and faith in its skills, are socially constructed through continuous reinforcement by this reference group of others. Teams with a precedent of winning have confidence in themselves based on their past achievements. Characteristically, these groups rarely abandon hope, because they believe in their ability to attain performance peaks and, ultimately, victory. Their definitions of the situation, even in the midst of misfortune, constitute a "winning attitude" that cognitively relegates poor play to a temporary status, thus keeping the spiral of focus, motivation, emotion, and arousal, so necessary to momentum, intact.

Conversely, teams marked by poor performance are imbued with a "losing attitude" that typically results from weak morale feeding off itself and spiraling downward. Through constant circular interaction these groups brand themselves with a demoralizing and burdensome stigma that is hard to erase. They feel they are losers, the coach acknowledges it, the press heralds it, and the record shows it; it is impossible to escape. When members of a team take such a perspective they are apt to continually invoke this identity, bringing the consequences of the self-fulfilling prophecy to bear. Coach Tom Landry recalls that when in its early years the Dallas Cowboys were an expansion team, it was plagued by this unshakable negative attitude:

> A lot of times our expansion teams looked like a million but they'd always beat us in the fourth quarter. You can build a team up all week, get them ready to play. They'll have a positive attitude, they'll get out ahead and be going strong. They go to the second half and all of a sudden they'll start hoping the game ends while they're still ahead. The result is that they're not continuing to dominate the game. The other team gets a break or two and then the expansion team starts saying, "Oh, oh, it's happening again." Before long the game is over and they've lost again [Jacobsen, 1978: B2].

Thus, the ingrained nature of these social definitions can often keep a group from reversing socially reinforced attitudes and hence momentum.

Social Setting

As the actual contest approaches, the ingrained social factors make themselves felt more acutely. Social interaction intensifies and generalized beliefs are expressed with more fervor. In part, this build-up is as socially contrived as the competitive event around which it centers. As Zurcher (1980) describes, diffused and specified arousal and emotions are orchestrated both prior to and during sporting events by a variety of "stage setters." From family to coaches, other players, cheerleaders, and even vocally active fans, participants in the setting provide cues concerning what kinds of emotional, attitudinal, and behavioral responses are considered appropriate. Interactional sensitivity and the mounting pressure of the occasion dictate compliance with these indicators, and players adopt (at least superficially) the proper premomentum pose. Once the game begins, this presentation of self begins to drop as self-consciousness gives way to concentration on play. Momentum can easily arise out of this constructed background, for even the slightest hint of impetus is seized upon by participants and spectators as an indication that the long-awaited spurt may be at hand. Everyone then responds with the overincited enthusiasm designed to propel all those present at an event (players, onlookers, and even the mass media audience) into the appropriate state of desired frenzy. Motivation, emotions, arousal, and even momentum are thus ritually constructed characteristics of sporting events, so framed and enhanced by the amplified focus and intensity of the social structure, social organization, and social relations of these contexts.

NOTES

1. See Lawther (1972) for an excellent and detailed discussion of motivation in sport.

2. Anthropologists have outlined and traced rituals, fetishes, and taboos in a variety of cultural, geographical, and social milieux. They point out both the functional and nonutilitarian meanings of these acts. See particularly Malinowski (1948), Radcliffe-Brown (1952), Rappaport (1966), Gmelch (1972), and Womack (1978).

3. I would like to thank Murray Davis for suggesting this concept to me.

4. See Goffman (1959: 197) and Bouton (1970) for further reasons supporting limiting the interaction between opposing ballplayers.

5. Theories of arousal have sought to explain the relation between arousal and performance, using pressure to represent arousal. Drive theory (Spence and Spence, 1966) proposes that as arousal escalates, so does the quality of performance, directly and indefinitely. The inverted-U hypothesis (Yerkes and Dodson, 1908) takes an opposing stance, disagreeing about the beneficial effects of unlimited arousal. At low levels of arousal a correlation between the two variables in confirmed, but optimal performance can only be expected to continue until moderate levels of arousal are achieved. As arousal rises above this point, the inverted-U hypothesis asserts that performance will begin to decline. Thus, humans can only function positively under low and moderate levels of pressure.

6. According to exercise physiologist Dr. James White of the University of California, San Diego, as expressed to me in personal communication.

7. See Tutko and Tosi (1976: 34-41) for a more complete discussion of these psychological and physiological phenomena.

8. Schwartz and Barsky neglect the somewhat controversial assertion that referees, too, are influenced by the clamor of the crowd. Many players, including some who have served as informal officials, support this contention, claiming that referees hesitate to call really close violations against local teams. Even NBA commissioner Lawrence O'Brien admits, "Basketball is a highly emotional game, and with fans' close proximity it's not humanly possible for officials to maintain total balance (Watkins, 1978).

9. Goffman uses this expression in a negative sense, indicating that people seek to avoid social faux pas. But I am employing it in quite the reverse manner, as an energy arouser.

10. See Tutko and Tosi (1976) for an interesting and more detailed examination of some of the psych out strategies considered here.

11. See Lyman and Scott (1970: 37-43), Goffman (1955: 213-231), and Polsky (1967) for further considerations of face, body, and con games.

12. Long an interest to ethologists, territoriality has been thought to be a basic biological instinct in humans and animals. Its major function has been to protect a given area and defend it from invasion of intruders. The analogy with sport, especially football, is obvious, as players fight to prevent outsiders from entering their "home territory." For more detailed analyses by ethologists and sociologists, see Portman (1961), Ardrey (1968), Hall and DeVore (1965), Goodall (1965), Wynne-Edwards (1962), Ball (1973), Lyman and Scott (1970), Weiss (1969), Goffman (1971), and Faulkner (1976).

13. The phenomenon of the second wind has been noted by physiologists for quite some time. See especially Cook and Pembry (1913), McCurdy and Larson (1939), and Astrand and Rodahl (1977). I have found no reference to data discussing the second wind from a sociological or psychological perspective.

14. Goffman introduces this term within the everyday life context. While his use of the notion refers to a desirable interruption of either accidental or purposive nature (as

when someone cracks a joke in constrained circumstances to "break the ice"), my application designates a less favorable occurrence for those being flooded out.

15. In almost all the interviews I conducted, respondents pointed to the greater proclivity for momentum in sports like basketball than in ones like baseball, thus supporting this general assertion.

4

MOMENTUM IN THE STOCK MARKET

While momentum has thus far been housed in the intensely personal struggle to overcome adversity and achieve excellence for an individual or group, I now examine its expression in the abstractly detached and objectified world of high finance. Focusing on the New York Stock Exchange (NYSE), the largest and most powerful free marketplace of the modern Western industrialist nations, I investigate the dynamic movement of stock prices as they soar, waver, and plunge.[1] Values reflect and sometimes anticipate the combined effect of international social, economic, political, and business conditions, as they are collectively analyzed and acted upon by groups of market participants. Here, the subjective processes of perception and interpretation intervene between objective occurrences and their effect on stock price values, leading to the creation of social meanings that can be widely shared or disputed. This context broadens the present study to include a macrodimension largely unincorporated in the previous area of inquiry, and illustrates the utility and feasibility of momentum's conceptualization on this level. Thus, as the inquiry into momentum in sport focused on individuals' and small groups' visceral physical performance, momentum in the stock market draws upon the actions, thoughts, and symbolic constructions of the masses. In moving upward to reflect this bulk and diversity, I selected the market because it incorporates and manifests the ascending spirit of individuals as they accumulate into groups, masses, and ultimately entire societies.

Examining existing theories of the market, we note that economists' models and laws of stock market functioning have tended to be highly rationalistic, ignoring the influence of varied human motivation and behavior patterns. Their approach to this area is grounded in classical economics' supply and demand theory, which postulates an equilibrium model of market pricing based on the actions and reactions of objective social, economic, political, and business forces. Individuals, where addressed at all, were assumed logically to follow motivations of self-interest, seeking to maximize their monetary gain wherever possible, especially in the short run (see Hutchinson, 1938; Hayes, 1950). A more recent outlook on the stock market has been taken by the random-walk hypothesists (Alexander, 1961; Granger and Morgenstern, 1963; Cootner, 1964; Samuelson, 1965; Malkiel, 1973) and their more radical descendants, the efficient-market hypothesists (Lorie and Hamilton, 1973). These modern economists have debunked the value of professional stock market analysis, claiming that a randomly selected portfolio has as great a chance of beating the market as any selected through professional advice. Their contentions rest on two assumptions: (1) that an adequate majority of intelligent investors have such complete knowledge of past and present information about companies traded on the Exchange (and that they have the ability to interpret this information correctly) that through their immediate trading actions they cause all stock prices to reflect the best current estimates of those companies' values; and (2) that investors are rationally motivated, excluding all behavioral goals but the short-run maximization of gain and minimization of loss. Economists' theories thus represent an idealized picture of perfectly knowledgeable and rational investors functioning in a perfectly competitive market.

A contrasting viewpoint comes from the crowd psychologists (Le Bon, 1897; McDougall, 1920; Freud, 1922; Mackay, 1932), who look on the type of crowd and mass behavior that occurs in the stock market as a descent to a lower form of human functioning. These "primitivists" believe that when united, whether by proximity or by a solidifying rationale, people fuse together into a psychological group of the lowest common denominator, thus unleashing the hereditarily baser instincts lodged in the repressed unconscious. Casting off society's normative restraints, the "group mind" is highly susceptible to the displays of charismatic individuals, easily led into extraordinary popular delusions and the madness of crowds. Crowd psychologists thus abandon the attempt to understand crowd and mass stock market behavior within the context of normality, considering it irrationally based and unpredictable.

Both of these perspectives, removed from their extreme positions, can contribute something toward the understanding of how momentum in the stock market arises. As the economists suggest, people do try to incorporate their knowledge of businesses and the world into their investment behavior and usually try to pursue a course of action that is fairly logical. But as the crowd psychologists have rightly observed, people often disregard their more rational urges, becoming caught up in the sweep of collective ideologies and losing touch with reality. By utilizing a sociological perspective, I hope to offer an analysis of how we can understand human market behavior and its resulting momentum swings as the reasonable actions of ordinary people acting within a given social structure, social organization, and social setting. Thus, as Rose (1966: 268) recommends, my study of market momentum focuses on a search for the myriad causes and effects of this human group behavior.

DESCRIPTION OF THE SETTING

Today's modern stock market is truly an arena of widespread participation, encompassing nearly all working people in this country. Both crowd and mass dynamics[2] can be found there, from the close contact, rapport, and interpersonal milling that takes place on the trading floor to the collective alignment of ideas and actions effected by people who are physically diverse but unified by a common interest.

Types of Participants

A great diversity can be found among stock market participants, ranging from active "pros" (insiders) to hesitant "lambs" (outsiders). Several groups can be categorized, each having a diminishing influence on price fluctuation, but combining to form the complex and shifting scene that makes this a distinctive arena for momentum.

Major institutions and their key directors are primary contributors to momentum; they have historically played a significant role due to the enormous financial power they wield. Included herein are banks, corporations, trust funds, pension plans, insurance companies, index funds, and hedge funds. The participation of major institutions ensures that a majority of Americans have at least indirect ownership of stock[3] through their fiscal affiliation with one or more of these organizations (via an insurance policy or company retirement plan). Institutional participants are primarily investors, leaving the bulk of their money tied up in stocks on a long-term basis, but holding a certain percentage for speculative purposes, to place in temporary situations where profit seems ripe.

Second in influence are the prominent individual entrepreneurs who play the market, often controlling large blocks of stock. Although usually not seat holders, they maintain regular knowledge of market movements and often act with a prescience that suggests inside information. This group has the latitude to encompass a broad span from business executives holding massive chunks of stock for corporate control to outstanding financiers speculating with their entire fortunes.

Stock exchange professionals are also heavily involved in daily trading, contributing significantly to the total percentage of transactions. Seat holders, from their vantage point on the floor, have the opportunity to buy and sell with each price fluctuation, making a profit on fractions of a point. Office brokers are active participants as well, keeping a steady eye on the market through their "broad tape" and computer screen.

Active outsiders can be considered semiprofessionals in the field, keeping abreast of the latest developments by sitting in the brokerage houses, reading news and economic reports, and calling their brokers regularly. Their interest is usually in speculation through properly timed sales and purchases, although they probably keep a more secure portfolio as well.

Finally, the least significant, as far as momentum is concerned, are the relatively inactive outsiders. These include the many people who have deposited surplus capital in the market for security, income, and possible growth with the national economy. But their timing and patterns of transacting are determined more by personal circumstance than by any but the strongest fluctuations, thus contributing a constant but serendipitous factor to movement swings.

The influence of insiders and outsiders is measurably unequal and makes its presence felt in different ways. Insiders are often privy to confidential information and can make their financial moves and affect the market before the general public ever learns that anything has transpired. By being close to the trading source, they also have the ability to react quickly to public information, reaping gains and unloading potential losers before the public can react, assess their options, and make a move. Finally, insiders often act stealthily, trying to disguise their actions so that others do not discover their plans. The result is that insiders have a vast effect on market fluctuations, although it occurs subtly. Outsiders, by comparison, are slower to acquire pertinent information, from both market and public sources, and produce further delays in action by not having the time or experience to assess and act on it promptly. However, when a mass of public sentiment does eventually build up it washes over the Exchange like a tidal wave, leaving no doubt as to the source, means, or reasons underlying its impact.

Collective Aims

As noted, these groupings of participants place their money in the stock market according to two general modes: *investment* and *speculation.* Investment refers to stock acquisition that is motivated primarily by a desire for security—for the dividend income that is accrued, combined with a hedge against inflation and participation in the national economic development. Favoring blue chip companies that pay a high yield, members of this class may adjust their holdings occasionally, but often maintain them intact from date of purchase until the time of financial need that forces dissolution of the portfolio. Investment-oriented purchases thus reflect a conservative outlook, channeling funds into "widows and orphans," companies that are universally acclaimed as pillars of the market and hence more apt to be chosen via sound business principles.[4]

In contrast, speculation consists of transactions undertaken for the purpose of capital appreciation, with the intention of holding the stocks on a temporary basis until an adequate profit is realized. Included herein are such practices as buying on margin (putting up a fixed percentage and borrowing the rest from an investment bank through a brokerage house); trading on options (securing the rights for several months to a stock's future gains or losses through paying only a fraction of the purchase price); selling short (borrowing stock from a brokerage house to sell, in the hope that the value will fall so it can be rebought less dearly); and arbitrizing (simultaneously taking a long and short spread on different sides of an issue to make money on fractional price fluctuations).

Unlike investment, which is sedate in nature, speculating evokes a thrill from the excitement and danger associated with the risk of great financial loss or gain. It resembles gambling in the enthusiasm and emotionality accompanying it, but the artificially created chance element found in those venturesome games is replaced here by the real hazards of tangible economic events and the vagaries of swings in collective belief. While speculators often cause price levels to depart greatly from intrinsic value, promoting the volatile "trader's market," they also serve as an "investment brake," limiting the outer ranges of momentum fluctuation by buying low and selling high.

Strategies as Collective Beliefs

Drawing upon and cross-cutting the aims underlying investment and speculation is a trio of trading strategies guiding market participants: *fundamentalism, technical market charting,* and *contrary opinion theory.*

The fundamentalist perspective, with its emphasis on concrete business soundness as the determinant of price fluctuation, dominates the rationale behind investment behavior. Espousing the credo, "true value will out," fundamentalists argue that the price of a firm's shares should reflect its real worth, as computed by current value, prospective earning, and dividend policy. When prices are accurately linked to earning potential, the flow of money will be directed toward businesses best able to utilize it, thus serving as an incentive to management efficiency and promoting the market's function as "optimal allocator" of funds (see Baumol, 1965: 35-60; Granger and Morgenstern, 1970: 1-43). Fundamentalists thus draw on a classical economics model of stock market functioning, regarding short-term price perturbations rooted in social psychological and technical trends as irrationally unpredictable and ultimately insignificant, to be nullified in the long run by the law of averages' tendency to restore equilibrium (true value).

The technical perspective provided by market chartists is more (although not solely) representative of the strategy powering speculative trading. Working from graphs of previous records, transaction volume, and current stock prices, technicians have evolved a statistical science aimed at predicting future price behavior. Their formulae are intended to aid followers in interpreting, measuring, and forecasting the strength of upcoming trends. Rallying behind their credo, "the market is the market," chartists form their predictions for the market by studying the general reaction to it. Thus, rather than speaking causally of social, economic, political, or business conditions accounting for market action, they attribute fluctuation to prior price patternings such as multiple "tops," "bottoms," resistance lines, and breakout points. For example, they commonly believe that if a price "barrier" has emerged through repeated topping at a particular level, once that barrier is passed, the momentum required to break through it will carry the stock's value considerably higher, until the next line of resistance is reached. They then immediately "put the word out" when such an occurrence transpires, warning people to buy immediately in order to profit from this anticipated swing. The success of these forecasts is thus integrally related to their function as "self-fulfilling prophesies"; in effect, they create movement by virtue of their very decree, as one securities analyst observed:

> Just because so many people believe the chartists' predictions, they may well come true. Over the last 4 years the whole stock market has been technically like ringing a bell, or a gun that sends off a 60-yard dash. It reaches a level where suddenly a whole school, and there are various schools, will take off. And just a wave of people—the following, the sheep—make it happen.

A "technical market," where the influence of chartists is pervasive, is favored by conditions both internal and external to the Exchange. Uncertainty and instability from social, economic, political, and business upheaval, coupled with the speculative traders' market, causes loss of confidence and investor flight. The departure of long-range, fact-oriented buyers exacerbates the volatility and meaninglessness of price levels, so that technicians, whose analyses are unhampered by a departure from fundamentals, thrive in influence. The whole market, then, tends to move in unison rather than with divergent showings in different stocks, amplifying and solidifying the momentum that develops. Expectations and reactions, unsteadied by real worth and the sober sagacity of classical analysis, begin spiraling with the mass mood. Prices are then open to sudden spurts, deflations, and reversals in accord with the irrational ascension and departure of hope, and the whimsical forecasting of technicians.

Contrary opinion theory draws upon the ideas of the previous two perspectives, providing market participants with a strategy for making individual decisions. Although contrarians admit the basic soundness of most fundamental business analyses, they assert that human judgment and communication are by nature problematic. At the point where original investment evaluations are made, the distortion is slight, but when this opinion becomes expanded to great proportions by market promoters, hucksters, and the excitement of popular sentiment, information and judgments increasingly lose their validity. The task of the contrarian is critically to assess where the repertoire of slogans and rhetoric have driven reason away, replacing it with mass, contagious irrationalism, and to speculate against this dominant market pattern (Neill, 1963; Thurlow, 1967). Contrary opinion theory thus weds the traditional fundamentalist approach to a critical analysis of the psychological dynamics of crowds.

Evaluating these competing ideologies leads one to recognize that they all have a temporal sphere of strongest validity: Technological considerations are more accurate for explaining short-term fluctuations, contrary opinion analyses recognize bubbles forming and play for their break over the mid-range term, and fundamental judgments usually come to fruition over a long-term span. Technicians can be faulted for their unbending rejection of concrete, factual influences, failing to consider the greater reality framing the market, that this is not a world apart but is limited and affected by tangible trends and occurrences. Yet in their concern to emphasize hard-core business causes, fundamentalists are also overzealous in denying importance to the technicians' and contrarians' implicit assertions that people respond to past and present market actions via a number of social psychological modes. Finally, although one can perceive a superficial resemblance between fundamentalists' and contrarians' focus on sound business judgments, a more profound compatibility actually exists between fundamentalism and technical market charting: Both are essentially "absolutist" (see Douglas, 1971), emphasizing the importance of totally objective criteria. Only contrary opinion theory attempts to integrate objective factors with the goal of this chapter: an understanding of how groups generate and are influenced by momentum in the stock market.

SOCIAL PSYCHOLOGICAL CHARACTERISTICS

In actuality, abstract political, economic, social, and business trends are only able to become translated into expression through the concrete realities of stock market functioning—through human beings buying and selling. As contrarians clearly recognize, it is human volition that fuels the dips and the recoveries of Wall Street, motivated by individuals' perceptions and attitudes about opportunities for gain and caution (rooted in their feelings of fear, greed, optimism, and so on). Social psychological traits provide a crucial framework, then, because all other influences must be filtered through human actors.

Interaction Patterns within and between Groups

The responsibility for making market judgments about the validity and timing of buying and selling is always hazardous, confusing the boldest and terrifying the indecisive. One result of this situation is the prevailing *sheep mentality*, the dominant stock market pattern of following others' thoughts and initiatives, thereby obviating the financial and self-esteem risk of personal decision-making. Although popular sentiment often resembles a confused rumbling of ideas and emotions, indistinguishable in origin or path of diffusion, two discrete models of mirroring can be discerned.

Following like others occurs on all levels and among all groups of market participants. This anxious conformity to the analyses and behavior of peers represents a clear manifestation of the human herd instinct.[5] In this pattern, the ideas being frenetically and emphatically passed around the group have no clear point of initiation; they somehow arise through the hesitant offerings and compounding certainty of the interactive process, through "groupthink" (Janis, 1972). Stock market outsiders are understandably prey to accepting the latest notion because of their general uncertainty and ignorance. The corporate mailings they receive are predominantly incomprehensible, and access to real business knowledge about firms is unavailable. Thus, they watch each other closely to ensure remaining abreast of any new information received. One broker described the scene created by these "board watchers" or "brokerage sitters" at his place of business:

> They all know each other and they stir up a great deal of momentum amongst themselves, dabbling in their penny and two dollar stocks, although they don't really affect the market. When one guy gets an idea to buy 1000 shares of ABC stock, either because he's heard a rumor, tip or "hot" story from someone else, he'll run up to the rail and yell his order across to his broker. Then the guy in the next chair will immediately run over to his broker and order 2000 shares of the same stock.

Stock market insiders are no more impervious to this suggestibility than those on the outside; in fact, they may be even more subject to its influence. People considered experts in the field are constantly interacting with each other to seek out opinions. Because market movement is tied to the volatile whims of human nature, they are often as unsure about trends and directions as their less informed compatriots. Thus, as one merchant banker remarked, they, too, hug the flow of the fold:

> People base their opinions on the prevalent attitude of others like themselves, being affected by group psychology and the momentum of the market. They're nothing but a bunch of sheep trampling after each other. If the market is weak for one week you'll find the overwhelming attitude among these "professionals" a pessimistic one. Similarly the most bearish

individual won't stick his neck out when everybody is thinking bull.

Professional managers of institutional funds are especially prone to this "fear motivation,"[6] panicking into the market and out of it as soon as they detect the slightest indication of this tendency among their colleagues. Their concern is not for overall profit, but for establishing a performance record that compares favorably with other money managers: "Relative performance is all that matters to me. If the market collapses and my funds collapse less that's okay with me. I've done my job" (Dreman, 1977: 110).

By circularly shadowing the beliefs and actions of like others, market participants display a variety of groupthink that represents the unified form of momentum's rise and diffusion. In merging their opinions so totally together that they feel released from the responsibility for individual decision-making, investors create a bond that unites their growing convictions into a collective belief capable of achieving and generating momentum.

The second observable pattern of interaction involves *copying opinion leaders*, where information and imitation diffuses from an inner central core toward the outer fringes. The center of this behavioral chain is a nebulously defined "they," who supposedly control the market with their inside information and immense purchasing power (Bond, 1930; Smith, 1967). Different theories hold that "they" have the power to move stocks and to split them, and that "they" always get the information first, or maybe even create the information. Although ascribed membership in this group varies with each opinion consulted, inside speculators and floor traders are carefully observed by others because of their propinquity to the actual base of price fluctuation, giving them the power to whip up a spiraling momentum through a frenzy of interstimulated trading. Securities analysts are also prime candidates to be "them," since they create the fundamental analyses that form the foundations of conventional wisdom. And recently, with the rise in power and influence of the institutional funds, professional money managers have been accused of being "them" (Smith, 1967: 208-215). These opinion leaders are all market insiders, working in the exchanges professionally and on a daily basis. From among their midst comes a continual stream of evaluations and pronouncements that are then transmitted outward, toward the buying public.

Large brokerage houses are prime carriers of this information, publishing the opinions and "buy lists" of their resident analysts and distributing them around the country to each affiliated customer's representative. These individuals then dispense to their clients advice on market conditions, theories, and the management of portfolios. Active and knowledgeable clients, in turn, distribute their information and opinions to friends not as abreast of the current market situation. Thus, copying opinion leaders includes following the opinions and actions of both the specific other (an analyst, broker, or trusted friend) and the generalized other ("they"). Here we witness the differentiated form of momentum's diffusion, different people gaining access to the outwardly expanding idea at different times so that they undergo the momentum-generating process individually, yet still contribute, through interaction, to the growing force of the investment belief.

Implications of These Behavioral Patterns

The communication patterns we have just noted affect the character and dynamics of the market greatly, generating a series of effects that influence the momentum of collective behavior and hence price fluctuation.

Following like others leads to the development and perpetuation of a circular arrangement, where, as people seek to follow the momentum of what is happening, they recreate it anew, illustrating the self-fulfilling principle. As increasing numbers of people are drawn to this burgeoning collective belief, a *bandwagon effect* begins to develop, amplifying any existing market momentum and propelling it to greater force.

The outward diffusion characterizing following opinion leaders yields another market dynamic: the *lag effect*. Here the ideology and excitement pass from group to group, affecting those on the outer fringes later than those in the central core. Once a belief in some idea has solidified, it can develop the self-generating and escalating force of momentum, so that withdrawing the initial source of drive does not halt the idea's progress; rather, motion continues, spurred by the acceptance it has gained, until it eventually coasts to a stop. Thus, when insiders stop buying and begin selling, outsiders continue their purchasing, as yet unaware that their leaders have switched tracks. Out of ignorance, outsiders are still propelled by the preceding but now moribund bullish attitude.

Conversely, an *anticipatory effect* is also highly evident in the market because of the *discounting* practice, where future performance potential is incorporated into the value level of existing securities. Prices, highly subjective in nature, thus go beyond reflecting a corporation's current worth to yielding an assessment of how people evaluate the firm's upcoming growth, earnings, and dividend potential. Any new information concerning either one particular company or the general political, economic, social, and business context which surrounds it, will immediately cause a reconsideration of the former expression and, through a flurry of buying and selling, be included in the measure of the company's stock value. Discounting in the stock market thus bears a resemblance to the anticipatory response we saw in sport, where before an actual event occurs, the individual, group, or social object experiences the arousal and thrust to momentum that that event would ultimately bring.

What we have, then, is a highly excitable arena where multiple groups and philosophies constantly interact in a complex and ultimately unpredictable manner. Moreover, because of the volatile nature of public sentiment, the prevalence of sudden shifts in collective attitude adds the *pendulum swing* to the overall pattern of price fluctuation caused by social psychological characteristics.

PRICE FLUCTUATION AS COLLECTIVE BEHAVIOR

> Born in a boom and cradled in a panic, the history of the stock market has been that of an alternation of booms and panics [Pratt, 1912: 349].

A volatile arena, the stock market swings back and forth between the extremes of high and low with a far greater frequency and intensity than does the surrounding business economy. This very fact helps to point out the role of nonfundamental factors in influencing the fluctuation of stock prices. When the market departs radically from the general trend of political, economic, and business indicators, it becomes particularly evident that the human variable intervening between these macroforces and stock price levels cannot be overlooked or taken for granted. In fact, as noted earlier, it is human group behavior which causes the market to fluctuate and achieve momentum. Price fluctuation must therefore be viewed as dependent on human group behavior, the real thrust to booms and panics. To understand the momentum of the market we must therefore look not only at objective price indicators, but also at the collective beliefs and actions of market participants.

The following discussion takes such an approach, offering a processual and phenomenological examination of how momentum ebbs and flows within the stock market setting. The overarching influence of fad and fashion on stock market swings is presented first, followed by a breakdown of market movements into two categories: the dynamic, sudden swings occurring within short time frames, and the slow, gradual developments arising over the long term.

Fad and Fashion

Earlier in this chapter we examined the general nature of this setting and the patterns of communication abounding within it. Unencumbered communication is of paramount importance throughout the career of a stock market momentum streak (boom) or slump (bust) because it transmits the flow of information and excitement that makes the growth and spread of generalized beliefs possible. Collective inclinations toward accepting new beliefs is heavily influenced by the vacillations of fad and fashion forming the background and tone that frame shifts in individual and group thinking. As one speculator advised,

> never underestimate the importance of fashion in any sphere of life, especially the stock market. It's what sets the attitudes of all the sheep on Wall Street who are busy running around trying to catch up with the latest trend.

The germ of a fad can come from a new product, catching the public eye and boosting confidence in its manufacturer. This can cause people to bandwagon a particular company's stock until the product's relative novelty wears off and the stock cools in popularity. Fashion can also strike an entire industry (as Mackay, 1932, describes for tulips in seventeenth-century Holland and the South Sea bubble of eighteenth-century England), possessing people with the unquenchable drive to invest in a particular commodity.

Fashion and fad can strike the very essence of investment behavior itself, bringing the effects to momentum swiftly and directly. The "go-go-years" of the late 1950s through the early 1970s provide an example of dynamically churning momentum and hysteria based on large-scale participation and extended endurance. The relatively quiet stock market succeeding World War II was followed by a period in the mid-1950s when people started buying securities once again. Soon there was not enough of the traditional "blue chip" stock to go around as more money and purchasers became available. One securities analyst described how a new phenomenon arose on Wall Street to fill this need—the "growth stock":

> It's patently absurd when you think about it to call any group of stocks growth stocks, like they're supposed to grow by guarantee and the others aren't, but the phrase caught on and new stocks appeared that started at $5 and went to $200; $10 stocks went to

$1000. People were literally waiting around and calling their brokers to get in on a new stock as soon as it was issued.

Active leaders appeared in the market to seek out new "high-quality growth stocks," commanding massive followings that pushed prices up by the sheer force of their self-fulfilling certainty. Stock prices soared from twenty and thirty times earnings to fifty times and above, expected to continue rising forever. These were thought to be "one-decision stocks": One only bought and never sold, since they escalated infinitely. But suddenly it became unfashionable to own growth stocks, and a new breed of "two-tier securities" were discovered that were considered qualities issues of a lower echelon. The dynamic momentum of the growth stocks shifted into reverse while the new group gained in velocity. These remained popular for a couple of years until their prices rose to unaffordable levels, only to be replaced anew by the next wave of mass interest. One stockbroker describes the transfer of momentum:

> Once the second tier had equalized itself with the blue chip stocks, suddenly a new slogan emerged from nowhere: "smokestack companies." Boom! That's what everybody wanted to buy. They were only selling at 3 or 4 times earnings while the others were at 40 times earnings. Then all the 40 times earnings stocks were sold.

But smokestack companies were replaced a year or so later as the pendulum swung again. In 1975 with the country in an illiquid situation and heavily printing money, the illogical decision to demand heavy dividend payoff emerged. A new group of companies promising "total return" and paying 11%-12% yields plus capital gains began an upward surge, collapsing the growth stocks. A securities analyst explained the changeover: "The new title gave total return stocks an identity with momentum. There was new confidence in one group and a lack of confidence in the other."

But total return stocks have also faded, replaced with today's fashionable "sound approach": market timing on the technical side, and trying to formulate all analyses with a computer. All the sheep are now busily trying to get in on the bottom of a narrow cycle and turn a quick profit without looking at the growth, dividend payoff, or even the fiscal solubility of the companies they buy and sell.

Thus, we see how the ordinary ambiguity of market participation is replaced by a shared belief that either the stock market as a whole or one part of it is becoming "hot" or dangerously weak, due to the wax and wane of different analysts' credibility and the shifting perceptions of situational market conditions. Slogans and catchwords that represent new ideas can be particularly important in generating initial attention to, and recurring recognition and (ultimately) positive acceptance of, a new market ideology.

Short Term

We find the most intense inceptions and reversals of momentum within the briefest temporal periods, since charismatic transformations generally occur rapidly.

Spark Start. Here, the precipitating factor most often takes the form of a spark start. These jumps, inaugurating both upward (bull) and downward (bear) movements, correspond to the impulses we witnessed launching momentum in sport. Spark starts in the stock market are characterized by "quick trigger reactions," a flurry of trades that quickly move a stock price higher or lower.

A spark start can originate from a number of distinct causes. *Charismatic events*, singly or in a series, can provide impetus to a momentum surge as people scramble to adjust their holdings in line with their now reformulated sets of expectations. *Public news* detailing developments of a less dramatic nature can also serve as a primary thrust, creating a wave of optimistic or pessimistic anticipation to ruffle market prices. Both of these precipitating factors thus yield a similar form of discounting, where the collective market reaction relies heavily on the subjective interpretation by individuals and groups of what effects a new development will produce, which does not always yield a consensus of opinion.

Collective behavior arising from the dispersal of *private news* results in a rather different pattern of momentum initiation. Here the unequal and selective dissemination of information forms a contrast to the instantaneous and universal availability of public news and events. Secret knowledge finds its way to the surface through complex leakage mechanisms based on interactional patterns that can be both inadvertent and purposeful, moving from the inner core outwards. The predominant type of private news is inside information about upcoming social, economic, political, or business developments. Corporate directors and executives usually have advance knowledge of such plans as stock splits, mergers, or dividend cancellations, and although technically they are legally prohibited from taking a position in the market because of this intelligence, or passing it on to friends, such occurrences are commonplace. Tips are another form occasionally taken by inside information, but these pieces of news, furtively passed from one individual to another (especially among brokerage sitters and other outsiders) are as likely to be groundless in fact as they are to be valuable. Nevertheless, they excite a flurry of emotion and prompt rapid buying and selling. Rumor is the most nebulous type of private news, mysterious in origin and variable in accuracy. Passed from one aggregate of people to another, it can turn out to be advance public news, inside information, deliberately misleading misinformation, or innocent falsity (Rose, 1951). In contrast to public news, where the startle effect hits everybody simultaneously and creates a marked surge that expends itself in one period of great intensity, private news seeps out in an alluringly mysterious way that slowly begins to gain attention. As people begin to wonder why a stock price is moving unusually rapidly, they may hesitate at first, but often try to follow the trend before it is announced publicly. The fascination of secret information can thus seduce people into exaggerated collective reactions, causing a greater short-term effect than had it been revealed instantaneously.

The result of this initial impetus on generalized attitudes is to transform previous vague suspicions into a more certain and specific belief by confirming ideas which have already begun to form. Any type of communication, whether face-to-face or via the mass media, can help to establish this common definition of the situation, structuring what had previously been an uneasy and unorganized glimmer of ideas. For the unfolding market bust, the unfocused anxiety is replaced by concrete fear of collapse, while in the case of developing boom, the fantasy of unlimited financial gain becomes attached to definite goals and means. Good news, though, never seems to produce as strong an effect as its inverse, partly because fear is a much stronger emotion than hope. Stock market momentum is hence always more intense in a bear plummet than during a bull rally, although the spread and concentration of movement is less noticeable during this initial impetus than during succeeding phases of the swing.

Carry-through. For all its drama, the spark start (as in sport) cannot be an exhibition of momentum without subsequent carry-through to develop the initial potency. This factor differentiates between a meaningless fluctuation and one that becomes significant as the starting point of a stock market movement. Particularly, there must be some secondary or derivative reaction that builds upon the primary impetus and carries the behavioral and hence price movement beyond it. The perception, generalized belief, and mobilization for action must spread to include an increasingly large group of people, through either the unified or the differentiated process. Only once this reactive procedure has occurred can the collective behavior be considered to have developed an internally self-generating force that will sustain its ascension to even greater levels of intensity and momentum.

During the carry-through phase we note the temporal separation of bull and bear momenta: Upward surges take longer to cultivate and instill, while downward plunges can escalate rapidly. Thus, intensifications of momentum occurring within the short-term framework are generally of the bear or bust variety.

In this situation, the impetus has created a negative atmosphere where optimism about the market's future stability is cast into doubt. Avid bears who chronically seek to profit by selling short can exploit an initiated spark and heighten it through speculation. Their active role of selling borrowed shares in order to drive the value down for later repurchasing thrives on the chaos and misfortune they create, fostering a general confusion, especially among outsiders, who are usually ignorant about such manipulative practices. As these investors become paralyzed by uncertainty and worry, the downward momentum builds.

Hindering momentum's rise are several factors that can contribute to the *abortion of carry-through.* Its absence can be purposefully orchestrated by an immediate suspension of trading: The NYSE's board of governors has the authority to suspend trading in a particular security or close the entire Exchange whenever it deems it necessary to salvage stability and prevent the rise of excessive momentum. Such actions occur regularly for individual stocks when inside rumors set off runaway prices that threaten investor security at the hands of wily speculators. Wide-ranging traumatic events capable of plunging the entire market into pandemonium, such as a presidential assassination, require dramatic action to restore calm. In the case of Kennedy, it took two hours for the governors to assemble the suspension and vote it into effect, but the market remained closed from that Friday until the following Tuesday. By that time Johnson had been sworn in and the transition accomplished in such orderly fashion that the entire decline was immediately recovered. Thus, the length of trading interruption judged necessary depends on the rapidity with which the underlying maelstrom or uncertainty dissipates.

Other stabilizing influences derive from the role of Wall Street clearing-houses and investment (merchant) banks that do heavy volume transacting with stock market participants and businesses in need of short-term loans. When adequately warned of an impending panic, these institutions possess the power to cut a potential momentum short:

> Nothing could have been more unexpected and terrifying than the shooting of McKinley . . . The next morning, before the stock market opened, a meeting was held at the Clearing-House, attended by the leading bankers, at which a pool of $30,000,000 was formed, and the announcement made that this sum would be loaned in the Exchange at market rates. Not a dollar of the money was used . . . the very assurance that the banks were ready and able to protect the market was sufficient to prevent any panics [Pratt, 1912: 366].

Further stabilization can come from parties sponsoring a particular stock. When major individuals, pools of people, institutions, or corporations themselves hold sufficient shares in a security, they cannot afford to let fluctuations develop that will gravely affect the worth of the company. Therefore, when the price starts to drop they will intercede to buy more shares and create a bottom limit. Similarly, when an upward sweep begins to burgeon, sponsors will offer part of their own holdings for sale to force a ceiling.

Turning from structural to active factors, the incident that sparked momentum can be effectively nullified by an opposing incident, as an experienced broker illustrated:

> Just yesterday, to cite a case, the President's Commission came out with a new report citing the extreme dangers of cigarette smoking. Naturally all the tobacco companies started falling right away. But then a tobacco industry spokesman held a press conference and accused the presidential aide of being an ex-smoker on a personal vendetta, and the stocks bounced back up.

Last, a spark start that carries a stock price higher can fail to develop carry-through because of the inherent instability of the corporation represented, the potential momentum faltering and dying of its own inadequacy.

Occasionally, even the preventative measures undertaken are inadequate to contain a fledgling momentum burst, and the precautionary actions taken are swept aside by the force of the raging tide. In October 1929, after the initial tremor of shock and horror had shaken the NYSE, a leading group of bankers under the direction of J. P. Morgan formed a pool, or "consortium," with $2.4 million available to render the fall more "orderly" and minimize the extent of the disaster. These funds proved to be insufficient, however, as the accumulated loss at the end of three weeks totalled close to $50 million (Bond, 1930: 196-201).

Emotional reactions to such rapidly born negative swings grip participants more acutely because of the *surprise* element accompanying the sudden shift. Initially, people respond with a loss of confidence, although they are likely to hold their feelings in abeyance pending continuingly similar performance along the same trend. With enduring tenacity, a dynamic market momentum can bring mounting feelings of fright and anxiety. Sudden and massive downward explosions, which leave little time for emotions and rational strategies to adjust, produce the most extreme trauma, in which suicidal despair can occur.

Sudden Breaks and Turnabouts. A sharp conclusion to a collective market momentum is caused either by a turnabout, by that trend's replacement with its antithesis, or by an abrupt break. Quick breaks and turnabouts are most characteristic of boom terminations, where the runaway bubble receives a sharp puncture and deflates. In some cases this resembles the loss of momentum occasioned by the interruption and intrusion that we witnessed in sport. For example, should something happen to remove a boom's chief promoter from the fore, the impetus he or she has built up could shatter and cause a momentum dissolution. For sudden stock market turnarounds, though, structural and collective preconditions favoring a new momentum have usually begun to build far in advance of the reversal's occurrence. As Smelser (1962) notes, only then can the antithetical collective behavior receive a true impetus from one thruster. One investor underscores this relationship: "Whenever you have a single event triggering a large number of events, that signifies that the trend was already set to go off without the precipitating factor."

Thus, what differentiates this terminating phase from the simple spark start is the collective movement-within-a-movement—the preparatory build-up of elements (often passing largely unnoticed) that will eventually contribute to a sudden, great readjustment.

The crash of 1929, Wall Street's most famous reversal, illustrates this point. This turnaround was preceded by spiraling investment trusts, holding companies, the reinvestment of paper profits, very high interest rates, and all the classical indicators of a "runaway boom." Under these circumstances many people, particularly the inexperienced public, lost sight of the demands and restrictions of real value in their expectation that prices would continue to soar unceasingly upward. Virtually all the people in the country were drawn into investing in the stock market as they saw their equally amateurish friends and colleagues becoming "paper rich" effortlessly. This group constituted what insiders call the "fringe element," that marginal component of ignorance and ineptitude that creates the final overblown peaks and valleys in the momentum curve. Unaware of the rational laws that usually moderate stock market swings, holding them within reasonable bounds, these nonparticipants continued investing indefinitely, based on their collective assumption that the market had no limit. Here the stage was set for the market to fall "of its own weight."

The transitionary phase serving as harbinger to the upcoming, short-term plummeting momentum is known as the "nervous market." An active agitation prevails, causing securities prices to rise and fall with abnormal frequency, the gaps between trades often exceeding the one-eighth-point norm. New highs are again set, only to fall dramatically between each one. No clear collective momentum toward any goal exists, but arousal runs rampant.

Finally, the break comes, sometimes induced by a specific impetus, although this is not requisite. There was no such charismatic external event on "Black Tuesday"; only the routine practices of Wall Street reacted, seemingly instinctively, to the overblown situation. Sensing the nervous market, many professionals had begun liquidating their portfolios to the wildly buying public. The overextension of bank loans for margin purchases and the skittish price pattern convinced insiders to turn bearish and begin selling short. Always the last to recognize and follow any new trends, the public was caught in the ensuing squeeze. The manifest cause of Wall Street's single busiest day (8 million shares were traded) was the widespread calling of loans by banks, investment trusts, and credit companies. This set off a chain reaction that instantly intensified the collective momentum as brokers had to put out margin calls to their customers. Before people had time to realize what was happening they had lost their profits and investments, flooding the market with even more "forced-sell" shares. With the departure of many professionals, an overabundance of amateur speculators were left to uphold the market, thus creating a situation where few knowledgeable sponsors remained who could have alleviated the crash. Spanning from October 29 to November 13, 1929, the fall lasted barely over two weeks but covered approximately 174 points in the decline.

Here we see how the conclusion of one market momentum can fertilize the roots of the next: when one collective belief and behavior pattern has pushed itself too far in a given direction (as greed encourages), the pendulum swing is apt to occur, replacing it suddenly with a mass flight toward the opposing inclination.

Long Term

Beyond the sudden momentum spurts, escalations and conclusions transpiring within a short-term time frame are those collective movements that take longer to build, establish their course, and terminate. These more protracted instances of stock market momentum are influenced by slowly unfolding, fundamental business developments as well as by the shifting pressure of collective attitudes. Within this span we note the power of both individuals and groups to generate the kind of reactions and actions that yield momentum.

Manipulation. A prime contributor to all phases of long-run momentum is stock manipulation. This term has two, often conflicting, connotations: It can refer to highly skilled and diplomatic speculators who use adroitness to conceal the intent of their trading so that others remain unaware of their plans, but it also denotes the fraudulent or deceptive operator who illegally or immorally influences price changes (Pratt, 1912: 364-366). Stock market manipulation of the first type has always been practiced by individuals, and represents the ideal of entrepreneurial acumen in a competitive setting. In the past, groups used to engage in the latter procedures, combining their resources to force prices to respond to a desired way. But the unified efforts of a few were so often successful in totally controlling market momentum, stopping it, and driving it at will to the detriment of all outsiders, that the SEC was forced to provide regulations outlawing such banding together. Due to the profitability in pooling funds to make vast purchases and "corner the market" in a given security, however, this behavior continues illegally on a smaller scale to the present time.[7]

In the preregulations period, associations known as "pools" were created for the purpose of controlling stock prices. Legal arrangements were drawn up specifying the members, their intents, and the procedures to be followed. Usually pools went "long" on stocks, secretly purchasing all the available shares in order eventually to create an "oligopoly," the market condition where demand exceeds supply. Various techniques would be employed to acquire a saturation amount of stock. First the "floating supply," or quantity of shares not held in long-term investment by individuals or corporate executives, would be gradually bought over several months by different pool members, seeking to conceal their accumulation. Then "shake-out" techniques, ranging from the spread of malicious rumors to temporarily flooding the market to drive prices down, were effected, in the plan to jar more stock loose from investors. With the scarcity of salable stock thus achieved, one member of the pool would begin offering purchase bids, confident that few sellers remained. This caused a tremendous momentum steadily to develop, driving the price to indefinitely high levels, where the pool then dispersed of their holdings, as previously determined. On rare occasions a pool would be formed to go short and seek an "oligopsony," or scarcity of demand. By discreetly borrowing massive shares of a leading stock to sell and then driving the price down with false reports, the pool members could repurchase their obligations at wholesale prices, before the misinformation was discovered.[8]

Cornering a market, although rare, can occur inadvertently as well. This usually happens to someone who wishes to make a large purchase for other reasons but discovers a shortage in the floating supply. After completing a partial acquisition, his or her offers to buy more bring a gust of momentum, the price escalating due to the mismatched supply/demand ratio. Manipulation, then, is the power to affect stock market momentum at will; once control has been acquired the individual or group can create a gradual movement, sudden rush, or total freeze.

The Gradual Rise. Over the longer time span we find the most common form of momentum's inception: the gradual rise. This is the predominant type of stock market activity after the irregular and meaningless fits and starts.

Various factors can contribute to the gradual onset of a collective stock movement, in contrast to those precipitating a spark start. Pieces of undramatic news that slowly fit together into a developing picture can quietly but steadily give rise to a collective opinion that fosters the gradual origin of momentum. From *business*, emerging labor troubles, overproduction, growing wage costs, increasing competition, government controls, and unforeseen accidents can contribute to downturn. A turnover of personnel encourages increasing confidence in a company's stock, bringing new vigor, spirit, and ideas; the steady growth of earnings and dividend issuances; products that show promise of mass appeal and profitability; and international promotion of the firm through personal appearances by the directors, stockholder literature, and advertisements in the mass media.

A second class of influences on slowly emerging momentum arises from the *social, economic,* and *political* realm. Favoring the growth of collective negative opinion and actions is an ever-tightening money situation, increasing unemployment, a further drain on gold, the nearing possibility of world war, and the gradual decline of the United States as an international power. Conversely, soaring personal incomes with accompanying consumer spending, growth of total census figures, and powerful funding for defense and aerospace programs beings a relaxation of budgetary controls and optimistic effect on upward price expansion. International as well as domestic trends can provide impetus to the gradual rise of momentum.

Although reactions to the stock market are usually highly emotional, the form of gradually developing momentum we witness over longer-term periods is more reassuring to most participants. Slow upward movements are somewhat expected, especially in periods of high inflation, thus arousing little response. Weak daily drops, even when they combine to produce an evolving pattern, also pass generally unremarked, particularly when contrasted with their sharper, more unexpected counterparts. This relative withholding of social psychological response can be traced partly to the ambiguity of gradual market motions and the overall hesitancy to pronounce a trend as developing until hindsight has made it clear. Emotional involvement is thus restricted to the dreams people have of wild and unfounded growth, and the very beginnings of more seriously based greed or malaise.

Intensification. As momentum begins to build from this moderate launch, it gains in potency and surety. Here, time is the main judge of the transformation from the inception stage to that where momentum can be considered established; the gradually ascending form shifts phases so subtly and smoothly that the movement can go unnoticed. One indication of advancement past the impetus is that external stimuli are no longer the only contributors to the growing price swing: *It has become a self-generating force that feeds off itself.* Social psychological patterns of collective behavior are triggered in an almost chain reaction, as the fear or greed generated further supports the evolving trend. This applies especially to indecisive or insecure individuals who follow a burgeoning momentum in a sheeplike fashion, hoping that its force will carry them.

Both bull and bear markets have their own intensification styles, complete with characteristic reactors that heighten the mushrooming momentum. In the bearish mode, the banks and credit institutions are the major swing factor, as they control the loans to people who buy on credit. They must keep their finger on the pulse of the market to determine when their own financial security is threatened by the growing down-trend. Their role, although decisive, is thus reactive to a momentum already in progess (as contrasted with the short sellers, who are active initiators). Calling in loans, which forces calling margins, results in the sale of more stock, exacerbating the falling market. Once wiped out financially by this procedure, individuals are unable to gain a new foothold in the structure, which might slow the process.

Here, the bland passivity of the wait-and-see attitude is abandoned and stronger feelings begin to emerge. Fear, insecurity, and loss of confidence intensify as people react with developing signs of individual and mass hysteria. Still, because of the gradual onset of this condition, they usually have time to recognize and accept the results of these financial momenta without being uncontrollably overwhelmed by them.

In the flourishing bull market there is no corresponding institutional or structural element playing the part served by banks. Smelser (1962) emphasizes the importance of key individuals who manipulatively promote certain investment issues, describing their role in leading the public to the widespread purchasing of a single stock or commodity as a major contributor to the intensification of stock market crazes. Whether charismatically manipulated by an outside individual or collectively generated through a groupthink process, the collective opinion of active market participants must gel with certainty into a favorable stance toward one investment strategy for momentum to become firmly established. At moments when this collective belief wavers or threatens to turn, a charismatic reification of its value can be provided by an unexpected stock split and extra dividend issuance, or by the flamboyant example of someone who has struck it rich via this investment means. These supplemental boosters act to "come through in the clutch" in much the same way we noted for sport.

What really transforms a cautiously optimistic market into a raging upward rush is the entry of the mass public into stock buying. People's suspicions and resistance to involvement in the capricious market are only overcome, though, as they observe opinion leaders climbing aboard the bandwagon and effortlessly earning paper profits. Hence, unaffiliated persons become involved in stock-purchasing in waves, as the collective behavior sweeps concentrically outward, encompassing greater numbers and types. Tempted by hope, greed, and the desire to "get in on a good thing," they add their money to the gluttonously expanding system, which becomes bloated by success and confidence. Then the fringe element, through their ignorance and gullibility, become infected with "speculator's fever" and bid prices beyond skyscraper limits. Indefinitely repeating technical formulae, they artificially inflate stock prices beyond what even psychological expectations can support. At the heights of the boom we see what Smelser (1962) calls the "speculative" phase, where investment for the purpose of high return becomes replaced by repeated buying and selling to capitalize on the skyrocketing appreciation. The practice of "pyramiding," or borrowing against the increment in a stock's value to purchase more stock, abounds, and this clinches the departure from reality that pushes prices near the "natural ceiling" level.

Gradual Ends and Reversals. Gradual finales, signifying the end of collective movements, frequently occur as a bust is terminating. These less precipitous abatements often overlap in character with momentum's leisurely incipience, especially in the final phases of the reversal, where the motion begins anew. Thus, the stock market revolves cyclically, never escalating indefinitely or collapsing in bankruptcy at the bottom, revealing the inherent presence of "tops" and "bottoms" where booms and busts end.

The bear market's slow finale sees momentum easing as prices continue to fall, although at a lingering rate. As heavy liquidation runs its course, people become aware that the market may be reaching its bottom. This discourages selling, since many now hope they will soon see a rise. Naturally, the insiders are the first to become aware of this trend and they may slowly begin to repurchase shares being released by the last outsiders. When the price level finally does reach the nadir, the complete halt to momentum is often accompanied by extremely low-volume trading, as one Wall Street broker described: "At that point the most pervasive emotion in the market is boredom: confidence has reached an all-time low, no one has a compulsion to buy or sell, and there is a general loss of interest."

The rebound from bear to bull is typically a slow, painstaking process. People who have incurred losses on the way down may be reluctant or financially unable to reenter the market and start the upward momentum. Here the fabled "bargain hunters" emerge to purchase valuable stocks cheaply, but their numbers are few and they are generally stock exchange professionals.

Bull markets finish sedately a smaller percentage of the time because the forces that pull the public in, breed an excitement and irrationality not easily contained. If the upward momentum has a chance to subside due to the influence of pessimistically portending external events that put a damper on general enthusiasm, price rises may be curtailed, permitting a gradual decline in fluctuation intensity.

The reverse thrusters that slow momentum's climbing force can also stem from within:

> The best professionals who earn their living on Wall Street must develop a "sixth sense" of when irrationality has run its course and when a sense of reason must return and make its presence

felt. They cannot afford to be professional gamblers, throwing themselves against the tide to gain the long-odds winner. A sure and steady income comes from being aware of how external and internal influences come together; that's how they're able to feel when the bull market has played out its strength.

Therefore a counterforce to the runaway greed of the public can emerge from the insiders who unobtrusively but steadfastly relax the excited momentum with the unruffling hand of calm selling pressure.[9] The intensity of upward movement thus brought to an end, the market will most often start into a pattern of gradual deescalation.

CONCLUSION

Having chosen the stock market for inclusion because of its macro range and broad base of participation, let us examine the influence of *different types of participant groupings* vis-à-vis the world of sport. While individual influence is vital in sport, it plays a distinctly secondary role in the market. Certainly, individual people enact the actual trades, compute the classical and technical analyses, promote lines of investment, and fill key decision-making positions in society, but their effect on momentum is forged only through the collective beliefs and actions of their followers. Organized groups of persons, another primary working unit in sport, can have significant influence on the rise of market momentum. This is most formally (albeit illicitly) evident in banking consortiums and manipulation attempts, where multiple resources must be pooled to attain the power adequate to either unleash or restrain breakaway movement. But for Wall Street, the unique thrusting force is the great hordes of overlappingly connected individuals, who, in pursuit of personal goals, provide an overwhelming (although often contradictory) stimulus that powers the abstract mechanisms of the market and directly creates the momentum in price fluctuation. Nowhere in sport do we see this widespread involvement; the great masses are tangential spectators to the flow of intensity. But in the market, even a previously passive observer has the potential at any time to join in the collective movement and add impetus to a momentum swing.

Perhaps this accounts for the *dynamic character of the stock market*; in contrast to many other arenas, it has a relative paucity of inertia. Whether the fluctuations be dramatic or sedate, enduring or quick, new influences are constantly entering the scene to keep it a vortex of churning activity. Yet these are unpredictable in essence; despite the best efforts of technicians and fundamentalists, the vacillations retain the human character of art, unable to be analyzed or unraveled on a purely quantitative dimension. They dance with the magic of vibrancy, spurred by an inner momentum possessing a life all its own.

When momentum is in evidence, its deportment is frequently capricious and roving, producing the pendulum swing previously discussed. Stock prices react to the whims and reversals of group perceptions and public consensus, oscillating from one extreme to the next. Although fundamental factors serve as the underpinnings of reality, they have no more influence over the dramatic, skittish movements of the market than people's actual perceptions of them, and this sobering pressure can be momentarily forgotten in the intoxication of excitement or fear. Thus, as history shows, the subjective trajectory of socially negotiated belief systems creates the basis for momentum in the market that often loses correspondence to actual events. Less shift occurs in sport performance than in this economic realm (although this perceptual phenomenon can also be found there) because of the impinging fundamental reality of the human body, which cannot be as easily overlooked or overcome.

Comparing stock market momentum with the models proposed in Chapter 2, we note the existence here of both the *explosive* and *placid* variety. The charismatic, highly emotional, explosive form is easily aroused by sudden or startling events. Sweeping crowds, it rapidly carries hope and dreams to exaggerated levels of elation or despair. But like its sporting correspondent, its volatility ensures its fragility, so that its potential for destruction also runs high. A more mundane and humble path is carved by the slow placid flow. Exciting remarkably little interest or emotion because of the extended accustomization period, gradually developed momentum resembles that performance state in athletics that has been achieved over an extended time from a history of victory or loss. Carrying with it an ingrained sense or lack of confidence, the steady motion continues in its path, less liable to instantaneous punctures or reversals. Yet, for both short-term explosive momentum and its long-term placid counterpart, all of the essential momentum components are recognizably present.

Stock exchange momentum can also take *positive* and *negative* forms, like the other area observed. But unlike sport, downside market motion is just as capable of propelling individuals and groups toward the goal of financial gain as is upward movement. Although athletic contests are not won in dejection and desynchronization, speculators can profit just as well during a slump by adopting a bearish outlook and selling short, as they can by buying long in bullish times. Positive and negative momentum thus becomes relative to the individual's position in the market. This divergence from sport is rooted in the departure from the simple two-party antagonistic situation. While the market is profoundly competitive, it is, as Hobbes described, a "war of all against all." Thus, people following contradictory investment strategies are mutually able to profit from a single market trend, freeing positive and negative momentum from their traditionally fixed opposing roles.

Last, contrasting with the overall nature of the collective behavior and associated market momentum found in booms and busts, we note that downward stock movements plummet about twice as fast as upward movements climb, doing so in far greater concentration: "A bear market, in other words, goes down by successive plunges in contrast to the steady, even when swift, ascent of prices in a general bull market" (Bond, 1930: 39). Here, a single bearish week may wipe out the gains so excruciatingly wrought over a year's time.

What are some of the sociologically causative elements underlying and contributing to this disparity? The first contributing dimension can be identified as differences in structural control between boom and bust momenta. Amounts and types of built-in controls inherent in their collective behavior, market mechanisms, and the greater society represent one arena where an obvious dissimilarity can be traced. For busts, the means of effecting control are primarily lodged in the early stages of its rise, in preventing its occurrence (by circulating calming information or redefining precipitating factors as harmless). Once the hysterical behavior has taken hold of the group, there is little that can be done to diminish its force. Those seeking to moderate a boom have a greater chance of success, however, because structural controls can be utilized, both prior to its rise and once it is under way, to help abate its intensity (e.g., legal and normative regulation designed to ensure the honesty of stock market procedures, such as regulations on credit extension, margin purchasing, and financial policies; laws against fraud, misrepresentation, and inadequate information distribution; and control through leadership by officially discouraging excessive speculation). Bullish momenta are thus liable to greater external pressure and restriction (Smelser, 1962).

The *organization* of collective behavior is another area of diversity that can help to explain the difference in boom and bust price movements. Busts, as we have seen, are often sparked by professional insiders who regularly engage in short selling and are exacerbated by the banks and brokerage houses that heighten the downward momentum by calling loans and margins. Booms although occasionally orchestrated by a few individuals, are dependent for their full strength on the entry of the mass public into the buying ranks. These two groups are clearly differentiated by their degree of organization: The insiders and major credit institutions operate with established lines of communication and known procedures for swiftly responding to familiar turns in the market, while the unconnected hordes of outsiders move haltingly and individually, unsure of which source of advice to follow. The tightly organized action of the bearish group thus enables them to bring their market results to fruition much faster and more surely than the uncertain disarray of those fostering rising prices.

A third contributor to this disparity is rooted in the human *emotions* which characterize market investment. Hope, the feeling propelling price ascensions, is a weaker and more fragile sensation than fear, the reaction driving values down. Confidence thus builds and intensifies more gradually and hesitantly than the gripping terror linked to potentially losing all. Therefore the foreboding certainty of pessimism, which sets in more quickly than budding, cautious optimism, causes the collective beliefs and actions fueling bust momenta to produce a greater concentration, intensity, and velocity than those forging booms.

NOTES

1. Some ideas, understandings, and examples are secondarily drawn from observation and interviews at the Chicago Board of Trade's Commodities Market, in a supplementary fashion.

2. According to Blumer's (1951) definition of crowds, masses, and their respective dynamics.

3. Although I use the word *stock* as an overarching term, this discussion is intended to apply to people trading in the full range of securities, bonds, and commodities.

4. Commenting on the pervasive influence of these foundational securities, one investor noted with sarcasm, "If IBM sneezes the whole investment community catches cold; if IBM goes to the bathroom the investment community has diarrhea, because it's the backbone of so many portfolios."

5. Many theorists liken the nonreflective contagion of ideas and emotions to the conduct of animal herds. Writing of the emotionality of the mass, Simmel (Wolff, 1950: 35) notes how "the softest wing beat, the slightest jump of a single animal often degenerates into a panic of the whole herd." And Blumer (1951: 170), too, cites the example of cattle building up to the intense fear and excitement of a stampede as illustrating a basic form of the circular reaction humans display.

6. Fear motivation is a destructive source of impetus that often yields the worst types of results. Being driven by a desire to avoid making mistakes, looking bad, or getting beaten focuses attention away from the positive goal and fixates it on that alternative most feared. It thus serves as one of the clearest starts to negative momentum, since like begets like, as was shown in Chapter 2.

7. Two cases are even now being prosecuted against the heirs of billionare H. L. Hunt, who have attempted (and succeeded in one instance) illegally to corner the market in soybeans and silver on the Chicago Board of Trade and New York's Commodity Exchange. Allied with family members and a pool of Arab investors, the Hunt brothers succeeded in acquiring more than 22 million bushels of soybeans in early 1977 (nearly one third of the market) and over 200 million ounces of silver by early 1980 (causing the Commodity Futures Trading Commission to impose such restrictions that the silver market broke and threatened to topple the entire stock market). See the *Wall Street Journal*, January 10, 1979, and *Newsweek*, April 7, 1980, for further details.

8. This type of practice was obviously more feasible in the days before instantaneous mass communication became widespread.

9. However, as noted, although it does occur, this type of gradual end to bullish momentum is rare, precisely because of the greed and exploitation possibilities that are ripe for insiders once the public is drawn into the market. As described in the short-term section, the more likely end to an inflated condition is the trader's market, where insiders rapidly make the turn from bull to bear (together, like sheep) and profit from the cupidity and ignorance of outsiders. The short sellers then deliver the final flow to send the momentum into instantly downside motion.

5

MOMENTUM IN EVERYDAY LIFE

In the previous empirical chapters I have addressed particularized arenas where momentum occurs, seeking to anchor the definitions and conceptualizations of momentum's abstract nature in concrete examples of real action that are situationally bounded. The present chapter moves to a different level of analysis, midway between the specificity of tangible occurrences and the high abstraction of generic theory. Here, I will focus on certain types of behavior that occur in everyday life, yet deal with them transituationally. My unit of analysis will be neither the concrete individual nor the human interactional process, but rather an ideal type representing a conglomeration of many persons' activities. By examining a few select forms of activity and cross-cutting their backgrounds of occurrence, I can simultaneously portray the dynamics of momentum experienced by the generalized actor engaging in these behaviors and evaluate the influence on momentum of diverse structural frameworks.

BIOLOGICAL RHYTHMS

Just as physicists considered motion fundamental to objects, so too is it for humans. Our lives are not organized around a static base, with each action taking us temporarily out of equilibrium only to return to quiescence once again. Rather, as Schutz (1967) asserts, we begin each day afresh, experiencing a unique though related sensation of vigor and alertness. Thus, our world is eminently replete with motion, continuing ceaselessly to ebb and flow. The cyclical nature of time permeates all facets of our existence as we move from day to night, summer to winter, birth to death. While a spate of research has been conducted on time cycles of plants and animals, notably little is known about human rhythmicity. Certainly, though, the innately rhythmical nature of life and human perception of it bears relevance to momentum, acting as a subtle detriment or support.

Contained within our bodies are biological clocks, those mechanisms that synchronize internal rhythms with the outside environment. Humans fluctuate primarily on a circadian rhythm, a cycle lasting slightly over twenty-four hours. Normally, environmental clues such as light provide signals to the brain's pineal gland and hypothalamus that stimulate release of the hormone melatonin at regular intervals throughout the day, keeping us in touch with outside, or objective, time. Secretion of this hormone, found in higher doses during manic periods and lowered during depression, is controlled by the chemical messenger norepinephrine (also known as noradrenaline).[1] Thus such ephemeral things as mood may also be related to the circadian fluctuation.[2]

Sleep cycles revolve on a circadian rhythm, periodically refreshing us during the dark hours so we can awaken regenerated in the morning.[3] Body temperature also varies concomitantly, reaching its peak at around 5:00 p.m. and its nadir in the early morning hours. Other characteristics with circadian fluctuation include blood pressure, respiration, eating and digestion, metabolism, and ultimately the strength and weakness of energy level.[4] Susceptibility to injury, pain, and illness is highest in the night and morning hours when our systems are slowed, while most people feel more alert and can perform best during the afternoon (Luce, 1971: 8-9). These clearly represent low and high levels of inherent biological momentum potential.

When removed from external time cues (e.g., clocks and light), people exhibit "free running": temporal organization based on the inner circadian pace. As this is slightly longer than the twenty-four hour solar clock, individuals usually extend their bedtimes slightly each day until they are eventually out of synch with everyone else. When brought back into society they must reacclimate themselves to normal time so that they dip and peak with the rest of the population.[5] This same "beat phenomenon" occurs when flying across long distances and is also referred to as jet lag or "phase shift." Often the greatest periods of intensity and accomplishment occur when time is ignored and work continues around the clock, provoking this syncopation. Free running and momentum are hence interlinked, both exhibiting a preference for continuous flow, uninterrupted by the enforced human norms of social time, which serve as a constraint by impinging on natural inner rhythms.

Time perception, another function of our internal clocks, is biochemically controlled and hence liable to influence by momentum. Our bodies become adjusted to receiving certain daily treatment at a regular time, expecting it without explicit awareness of the hour. Likewise, we develop a feeling for time passing and can often estimate the length of time intervals. But the passage of time is not experienced evenly by all people. Piaget (1966) reports that children, for example, seem to feel time more slowly, are always impatient when waiting for a set hour, and sense the seasons and years as longer than adults do. This is related to the greater speed of their internal rhythms (metabolism, heart rate); they fit more of life into each day. A similar condition can be induced by drugs, where people, when asked to tap at even intervals, accelerate the tapping at the peak of the drug state. This "time contraction" undoubtedly occurs at the height of momentum states as well, because the bodies' internal mechanisms get stirred up by the excitement of intensity. Thus, one loses a sense of time when performing feverishly.

Additionally, the notion of time, and hence momentum, has been classically recognized by social scientists as influenced by subjective perspectives. People in different occupations utilize diverse benchmarks to note their relation to time passage (Lyman and Scott, 1970: 189-212; Roth, 1963), while whole societies may be classified by the "rhythms, pulsations, and beats" that characterize them (Sorokin and Merton, 1937).

Time, rhythm, and pace are important elements of momentum. People, who must deal with their natural subjective clocks as well as more objective standards, find it problematic when the two do not mesh. Lodged, as we are, in a world of rigid routine, the daily ebb and flow of each individual's bodily and social psychological rhythm must often be sacrificed. Yet this convergence is highly influential to mood, resiliency, productivity, and hence momentum. Some attention has been given to the cyclical nature of life in the recent vogue of pseudoscientific biorhythmic charting.[6] Although the stark simplicity of this theory renders it implausible, the underlying idea has value. By recording basic undulations in feeling throughout the day over a span of months or years we may someday be empirically able to forecast optimally favorable periods for developing momentum.[7]

Understanding the biological capacity of human physiology as it relates to rhythmic cycles provides a fundamental background for analyzing momentum. When elective behavior runs counter to innate tendencies, productivity and velocity may seem mystically thwarted. Conversely, an unexplained surge in strength and power may be rooted in accidental or instinctual convergence between subjective and objective periods of force. Only by utilizing our knowledge about timing, perception, rhythms, and natural peaks can we plan a behavioral superstructure that respects the way we perceive our biological cycles and achieves the dual, internal and external impetus to momentum.

TASK ACHIEVEMENT

Given this background, let us now look at the activities people undertake and how their progression is influenced by the dynamics of momentum. The instrumental sphere of work is my first focus, where I will examine the task of academic writing. I will chart momentum's flow by stages throughout this ideal typical, abstracted undertaking, extracting generalized elements of relevance to performance levels, intensity progression, and the relationship between input (effort) and output (reward or accomplishment).

Anticipation

Germination, the necessary first component of all tasks, occurs in the mind of the creator largely as a result of his or her communication and social interaction with others. This nascent stage, where ideas are originally born and cultivated, serves as a prelude to the further outgrowth of particularistic behavior.[8] For the academic scholar, the inspiration to attempt a new piece of writing may stem from his or her experience, curiosity, world developments, challenging theoretical issues, or other literature in the field. Once the initial idea is implanted, a plan must be formulated to ensure its progression to the point of culmination. Visualization of the entire project, as we noted in sport, aids its eventual realization through a mental and musculoskeletal rehearsal of the projected activity.[9] Intellectual preparation thus generates activation, stimulating the complete readying process of emotional and physiological arousal. Here, the academician pensively considers alternative empirical and conceptual theories and approaches to the topic. Although internal intensification and morale development (which often involve the greatest anguish) are proceeding, this stage of achievement is often misinterpreted by outsiders as "spinning one's wheels," because the high degree of effort expended results in little perceivable progress toward the goal. If the project were abandoned before the onset of forward movement, occurring for instance as the result of other commitments superseding this one, it would normally be dismissed as unproductive. Only in retrospect is this recognized as the first phase of momentum: *preparation.*

Inchoation

Getting started, the most difficult part of an undertaking, necessitates a transition from the passivity of motionless contemplation to the realm of active manipulation.[10] Conquering this inertia requires the greatest thrust of impetus, because of the undiluted resistance of complete immobility (vis-à-vis this task). Reminiscent of overcoming stock price barriers, the "threshold phenomenon" resurfaces, ensuring that once adequate force is accumulated to overcome an obstacle, the strength of the impelling effort will carry motion further with minimal difficulty. This *impulse* thus becomes the first externally visible sign of momentum.

Actual exertion at this point often involves further preparatory groundwork: negotiating with others for time, materials, space, and money; discussing ideas with colleagues for the purpose of getting feedback; and establishing a framework and pattern that will shape future productivity. Energy flow is still predominantly outward as the project remains unrecognizable ("on the drawing board") and frustration runs high because of difficulties encountered from self, others, and tangible obstacles. "Tunnel vision" is commonplace, since the needs of an infant project are consuming, demanding one's entire attention. The rewards of imagining the completed task, readily obtainable during the anticipation phase, fade now as mental effort can no longer be spared. From the arduous point of commencement through the continuing difficulty of foundational construction, then, inchoation represents the most grueling work, greatest output, and least amount of gratifying input.

Taking Shape

Once action is under way, progress begins to proceed more smoothly, as preconceived ideas solidify and plans of execution unfold. Having broken the strongest resistance barrier with the primary impulse, the academician continues to erode all forces opposing his or her developing momentum by pressing ahead with the writing. Usually felt as a difficult chore at first, the outpouring of words begins to flow more smoothly and easily as an inner rhythmic synchronization develops. Establishing a routine for accomplishment leads to the habituation of regular forms of action, yielding ritualized behavioral patterns. While such *repetition* alone does not produce momentum, its role is important, because familiarity permits the pace of performance to accelerate, simultaneously freeing the conscious mind to tackle more complex problems.

Finally, creation begins to catch up with inspiration and the great disparity between input and output nears equalization. A rounded feedback mechanism emerges, rechanneling the gratification resulting from achievement to facilitate the manufacture of raw energy. As abstract images begin to take shape, this further generates great satisfaction, aiding concentration and lifting spirits. With this positive attitude dispelling inner resistance, the working routine functioning to resolve external impediments, and a circular return system recycling and boosting effort, we find the greatest increase in momentum attained in a *carry-through* phase. Yet, precisely because of this precipitous rise, people are almost afraid to divert their focus for an instant, lest everyday activities interrupt the flow and raze intensity. Furthermore, despite the escalation, performance still lags behind expected levels.

Plateauing

Upon attaining a satisfactory rate of productivity, writers generally relax the push to accelerate and turn all energies toward task completion. With concentration and time allotment adequately ensured, academics settle into a pattern of working hard, which may vacillate from time to time but generally remains steady. By now, an efficient operative procedure is, in effect, ensuring that maximum potential is elicited, utilized, and returned for the greatest gain. Input and output have finally achieved complete par, remaining consistent for as long as is desired. In a lengthy task, such as writing a book, the majority of work is completed at this stage, where aspiration, dedication, and fruition run high and focus is clear and concentrated. For articles or papers this can be a more fleeting step, attained briefly, only to be relinquished shortly thereafter. Regardless of duration, plateau periods maintain a predominantly steady rate of motion, righting disturbances from both inside and out, achieving progress toward the goal, and witnessing a uniformly optimal degree of effort and satisfaction.

Nearing Completion

Altering the finely tuned balance of stabilized propulsion, the approach to the end can provide an excitement previously lacking in the project. Suddenly, those tunnel-visioned in the vivid present recapture an image of the future, and the dreams they had of their completed work appear within grasp ("the light at the end of the tunnel"). Anticipating the culmination and prematurely beginning to experience the joy and relief of consummation has a twofold effect on the nature of input: Effort becomes easier with the perception of augmented reinforcement and invigoration, but simultaneously a letdown factor intervenes, releasing all of the natural exhaustion that has been building up continuously, but which has been held in abeyance by the pressure to achieve. Thus, while the individual begins to ease emission of new energy, performance levels may continue as previously, buoyed by the behavioral system in operation, which fuels itself by ingeneously utilizing all available resources. Such a pattern can carry the academician in a "coasting" posture completely through the finish, where he or she ceases to need any further internal pressure to write, being almost drawn toward the culmination by the promise of goal attainment and a respite. This is facilitated by a change and easing of the work load: The bulk of creation complete, only perfecting details, promotion, and distribution remain.

At the very end the slackening effect is likely to reverse itself, as the individual becomes totally immersed in the excitement of the original dream and thunders with "remomentum" toward its realization, like the runner sprinting to the finish line with a final "kick." With all impediments finally removed and interest and effort rejuvenated, activity culminates on an upswing in all dimensions: exertion, rhythm, tempo, performance, results, and satisfaction.

Denouement

After final touches, productive activity ceases and the task can be considered officially completed.[11] Having heavily depleted all energy reserves throughout the project, especially in the terminating push, the academic is now ready to relax, deaccelerate, and enjoy a recuperative rest. But such an accumulation of invigoration does not disappear instantaneously; it lingers on, buoyed by two circumstances: First, the deescalation of movement so ingrained can only be accomplished gradually (analogous to finding one's "land legs"). Second, the pride of creation, coupled with the relief of ending, produces stimulation that temporarily perpetuates arousal. Intensification (especially psychological) is thus sustained well past the point where impulse has ceased (a trademark of momentum).[12]

The most significant aspect of a task's career for this study is the *lag effect* manifested in the syncopation between energy fed into production and the level of performance output achieved. At each stage the momentum corresponds to the effort invested during the previous period, regardless of current input. Beginnings and ends illustrate the lag most clearly, where there is initially a highly aroused drive without discernible motion and later a relaxed inactivity characterized by performance ease. This time delay stands in contrast to the immediate gratification we shall observe in affective relationships as well as other, unstudied activities. Some forms of everyday life thus require an *incubation* period to bear momentum's fruit.

AFFECTIVE RELATIONSHIPS

Romantic entanglements represents another major sphere of most peoples' everyday lives, yet stand as a contrast to the usual rationality of instrumental, task-centered action. Falling under the rubric of sentiment and feeling, they are highly subject to the ebb and flow of emotion. We have seen how the stages of a task can be clearly delineated and analyzed in terms of its internal and external dynamics. I offer the example of affective relationships as another critical aspect of everyday life momentum, in part because they cannot be predicted like the flow of task achievement; there are many paths and forms a romantic affair can take. By presenting and discussing the major ones, I hope to illustrate another way the momentum process can be embodied in human social behavior.

Affective relationships possess an importance in everyday life that need not be underscored; elemental happiness or despair may hinge on their presence, absence, or quality. I envision them as an integral part of the stream of life, ranging from the "continuous," long-term entanglements of marital partners to the "episodic," temporary affairs of intense passion but abrupt wane.[13]

Prior to the onset of a relationship, if the prospective participants are "ready" to get involved, their emotional states will be better prepared to accept the probable stresses as well as the joys that inevitably arise. If either party is entangled, either connubially (in the broad sense) or by inner problems, they may be unable to offer themselves completely to another. As one who had suffered a severe heartbreak explained,

> It took me a long time to get over Chuck. The feelings that remained tied me to him still, and the hurt that I went through

soured me on looking around at other men or even thinking of getting involved for many, many months.

"Mutual openness" (Goffman, 1963: 131) is hence the optimal precondition for individuals seeking a relationship, as it signals a removal of the inertia-enforcing solitude.

Liaisons may vault to a spark start, typified by the idealized "love at first sight." Typically, only people previously unknown to each other exhibit this resounding escalation of momentum, attributed to an intangible attraction based on body chemistry. Romantic magnetism can be rapidly enhanced or promoted, however, by certain deliberate actions. Nonverbal contact, with its standardized norms of distance and etiquette, enables people to show their attraction for each other by subtly departing from established practice. Ritualized interpersonal modes of conduct like glances, spacing, and other "opening signs" (Goffman, 1963: 91-95, 161) can be either obdurately performed, scrupulously adhering to polite social norms of distance, or daring breeches of custom, enabling interested parties to "come on strong." Unspoken communication thus has the advantage of constituting a highly personal encounter without the associated risk inherent in verbal interchange, so that if reciprocal interest is not displayed the initiator may back down without embarrassment. Hence, by setting standards for proper impersonal behavior, social codes provide cues for the interpretation of deviations from discretion that can launch a budding relationship, thereby reversing their normal role as hindrances to momentum.

A *gradual rise* in romantic intensity may occur among people who are familiar in varying degrees. "Sight acquaintances," known to each other only by repeated passing glances, may escalate their relationship cautiously and inconspicuously in the absence of a formal introduction. The lengthy opportunity to "check one another out" and mutually fantasize about each other leads to a moderately paced acceleration of relational momentum until such a time as a "chance encounter" can be arranged. For those already acquainted, bonded by platonic or professional ties, the drift into more intense sentiment comes the slowest. Standing as an intangible obstacle, their previous affiliation must be broken down in stages for the new one to emerge:

> Laura and I became friends when she was still living with her husband. At work, I'd just go into her office and talk to her for long periods. After things started getting rocky between them I could feel the attraction between us, but because we were friends neither of us made a move toward the other. Only bit by bit did our old friendship relationship break down so we could become lovers.

Thus, a past or current attachment by one party is often a confounding variable that disintegrates either just before, during, or after a link is formed with the new person. Here, too, nonverbal contact can be instrumental in revealing "change signals" (Goffman, 1971: 203) that signify the relational transmutation to those involved and to perceptive others. *Prior familiarity and the rapidity of momentum escalation can thus be inversely related.*

Diverse patterns of cautious feeling-out prevail during this early interval of rapport-building, where each person is interested but afraid to let the other know. Defensive sparring, a form of hard-edged flirtation, is customary. Humor plays a key role, allowing emergence of the genuine feelings that one is hesitant to express sincerely for fear of condemnation. Once again, microsocial barriers shaped by etiquette, social norms, and morals (taboos against "kissing on the first date" or ruining one's "reputation") intervene to restrict spontaneity and restrain the growth of intimacy. Arousal, heightened by anticipatory sexual titillation, keeps pace with the development of the relationship, evolving simultaneously in both participants and leading to fledgling momentum.

Eventually, mutual interest is ascertained, through any of countless courses, transforming the delicate dalliance into something solid. A tangible relationship can truly be said to originate here, often being traced by participants to one specific symbolic act.[14] With the bond of commitment established, any satisfaction derived from the liaison will circularly feed back, immediately strengthening it and invigorating the momentum.

From here on, the games of hiding interest are over (although others continue) and the two people begin to reveal their inner selves to each other. Trading progressive pieces of information and sensitivities creates a comfortable emotional climate where security and affection can thrive, accelerating movement into a rapid upward spiral. Courtship rituals also escalate in both sequence and pace, moving from occasional dating and physical contact to regular companionship and serious sexual relations.[15] Sexual intercourse provides the biggest single boost to confidence and bonding, complementing the mental unveiling with a complete intermingling of intimate physical beings. Full infatuation usually results, making this stage the most passionate and intense in all respects (while still escalating greatly):

> Our relationship had been progressing along nicely, although there was nothing extra special about it in the beginning. But when we made love for the first time, with the sun beating down on our naked bodies, everything suddenly changed. We were both overwhelmed by the intensity of our passion. It was love at first fuck.

After the initial surge of excitement and discovery has settled, the couple normally looks ahead to assess their potential future together. An evaluation of compatibility, mutual interests, and common values is made and discussed. Momentum's upward rush may slow here as the focus becomes more serious and a major turning point is reached. Key confrontational conversations can lead to "shake-ups" (adjustments), "break-ups" (separations), and/or "make-ups" (solidification).[16] A decision to "cool out" the relationship can come from the intervention of outside complications, the rise of inner friction, or the sheer diminution of impulse due to loss of interest (either one-sided or joint). After this, termination is usually not long in coming.[17] Finding each other's companionship enjoyable but not capable of reaching greater heights leads to a steadying of velocity and momentum, to be maintained on a sensory but meaningless plane. Couples can continue in this fashion until a change of status is introduced from without or the frustration of limited satisfaction builds to a point initiating dissolution.

> I was very interested in Wendy at the beginning of our relationship. Things between us intensified for awhile but I knew she had an out-of-town boyfriend. This bothered me and we eventually had a long talk about him and us. It became clear that she wouldn't give him up, so I knew we had no future together. Things dragged on for awhile but they slowly fizzled out as we both lost interest in a "nowhere" relationship.

However, when the right combination of interpersonal indicators is present, a decision to work toward the apex of momentum (monogamous commitment, in our society) ensues. Relational performance once again surges, bolstered by this positive resolution to the questioning of mutual concern.

Further development of the relationship is marked by vicissitudes in its momentum. Dominance and submission struggles emerge after the blinding infatuation has faded, opening participants' eyes to each other's weak spots and their own egotistic needs and desires. Role formation involving superordinate-subordinate stratification (i.e., benefactor, mentor, or initiate) may dissolve or shift as initial mystique is replaced by familiarity, an inexperienced partner gains knowledge and practice, and self-confidence supplants withdrawn timidity. Churning interpersonal changes and fluctuations may diminish in magnitude as the interlinkage endures, but even in the most steady relationship they never disappear completely.

Eventually the individuals achieve greater familiarity with each other and their behavior becomes more mutually predictable. Relative novelty languishes[18] and the process of falling in love culminates with momentum affectually stabilizing at peak performance level. Once again we witness the emergence of a ceiling effect, felt later in some relationships than in others, which affirms momentum's inability to escalate indefinitely. But acceleration does not give way to the even keel of inertia despite the near plateau reached. Just like stock market swings, which are always entangled by complicating side vacillations, a basic love relationship is constantly beset by problems, depressions, exhilarations, conflicts, reunions, and resolutions that keep it in a moderate state of flux. Moreover, a strong, loving bond with high momentum is not sustained by two people who have experienced infatuation and expect to coast on the strength of that initial outlay. Rather, continuous, active, and renewed effort must be made simultaneously by both parties to keep their relationship *"cruising"* at peak quality:

> Intimates may find it difficult to keep each of their organic rhythms in tempo. When these physiological pulsations get out of phase, each intimate will find that, in order to accommodate the other's rhythms, he must readjust his own. In other words, when intimates are out of step, either each will have to compromise his own desires to a large extent or both will have to compromise their own desires to a small extent in order to reestablish their common cadence [Davis, 1973: 200].

A communion thus refreshed and reinvigorated grows throughout the years, producing parallel change in participants as they age and develop.

In some cases the willingness to summon the energy needed for this level of intensity diminishes over the years, as (commonly) marital partners becomes less focused on passionate aspects of their life together and come to rely on each other more for companionship and security. Ingrained habit fosters their continuing preference to remain interlinked, as well as do mutual ties and affection. But the performance intensity of their bond subsides to a lower-level plateau where it may continue indefinitely. This *routinization of momentum* corresponds to the bureaucratization of the relationship, held together more by form than by content (although still not an empty shell):

> When we first met things were so different between us. He used to tell me all the time how beautiful I was and shower me with attention. Now we've got three kids and his father living with us,

> and he teases me in front of my friends all the time about how fat I am. I hardly see him because he works late at the shop most nights. We still make love and are very fond of each other, but the sparkle that was once there is definitely gone.

From this slightly lagging state where feelings and momentum have waned in intensity, a second wind may emerge. This reinfusion of sexual attraction and love is often sparked by some crisis that threatens the life of one or both partners or threatens their relationship. The jolt causes them to reexamine the very roots of their existence and realize the things most important to them. A combination of inner needs and rational decision-making causes the couple to reach out, as they suddenly appreciate how much they have been taking each other for granted. Feelings of affection then overwhelm both partners, thrusting them sharply to the greatest heights of peaking.

> I was afraid to tell him about my affair—afraid that he'd never trust me again and that he wouldn't feel the same toward me. I was afraid of losing everything we had worked for. But when I did tell him, his response was to love me more. He was so afraid of losing me that his feelings grew stronger than they had ever been. We put everything else aside and spent the next month making love with a sexual passion we had never known before. I think the waves that overcame us then were more intense than any we had ever experienced, as we fell in love all over again.

This relational second wind can often surpass the first falling in love in the heights of ecstasy and depth attained. The partners are more mature, have years of experience and personal history invested in each other, and have overcome feelings of ambivalence or diminished interest to achieve this second peak. They treasure it as a second chance or new awakening.

For those liaisons that do not endure, the transition into decline may be either subtle or sharp. Gradual deteriorations are usually caused by intrinsic failings, as the couple finds each other's company increasingly less satisfying. After coasting for a period (which varies, depending on the intensity of the original bond) on the strength of their structural affinity (heightened by social norms discouraging dissolution), two individuals may find their remaining ties considerably weakened. Sharp decelerations in momentum are often prompted by confrontations stemming from outside sources. Such intrusions into the private sphere may promote loss of trust, brutally slicing through pledges and obligations. Ultimately dissatisfaction becomes mutually evident, sending momentum negatively spiraling.

When psychological damage incurred from the relationship outweighs its benefits, participants begin preparing for the inevitable pain and difficulty of the break-up. Conflicting microsocial leave-taking norms both hinder and facilitate a dissolution by insisting that one party should politely wait to end the relationship until the other accedes, while concurrently maintaining the rights of departure owed individuals under tactfully managed circumstances (Goffman, 1963: 110). Although an amicable separation helps to ensure behavioral compliance with etiquette, the depth of emotional attachment involved often destroys rational thinking and acting.

Abrupt initiations of the termination process particularly inflame shocked, hurt, and angry feelings, leading to fierce interpersonal struggles and renewed arousal, albeit of a negative thrust. Almost invariably introduced by one member, the sudden decision to seek freedom is often prompted by external stimuli. The trailing interpersonal intensity is thus dramatically lifted to produce a permanent quiescence. Since the other partner rarely manages to save or prolong the affair, he or she is left sinking rapidly into the morale and performance depths of self-pity and despair, while the instigator of the split can recommence life from a positive stance.

In contrast, separations of *mid-intensity* and duration characteristically draw on the reciprocal deterioration recognized by the dyad. Conversations, centering on mutual dissatisfaction and "working things out," have proceeded for some time, but to no avail. Both parties, unable to terminate the relationship since some lines of communication and affection still remain, make the final cut by unconsciously "creating a crisis" (Rasmussen and Ferraro, n.d.) that will force them to split. Situations previously accepted become redefined as unbearable, and irritating behavioral aberrations are aggravated to provide an impetus. Reacting to each other to build momentum, the couple eventually reaches a climax where one or both parties perform intolerable acts, thus necessitating and justifying a severance. Unlike the abrupt dissolution, this parting leaves neither partner as pleased or as distraught, since both are moderately happy to be released but bear wounds inflicted during the break.

Extremely *gradual* finales to relational momentum may involve uncertainties and trial separations that drag out lengthily. Here the greatest resistance factor is present, so that people are unable to muster enough vitality to achieve any animosity. Pursuing their separate existences while remaining formally united, their affiliation is marked by indifference. In some such cases people are never able to risk the change and insecurity divorce would bring and continue together until "something better comes along." Others arrange for their spheres of life to diverge very slowly, moving into different interests and residential locations.

Break-ups thus bear many resemblances to take-ups in the resistance pressure hindering any major change of status or movement in life. Obviously the restrictive encumbrance of dissolution is amplified by the social institution of marriage; relationships not cemented by this bond or by offspring may be dissolved with comparative ease. Informal social norms combine with legal regulations to exert a conservative influence here, pressing for maintenance of the relational status quo for as long as possible (although with the present weakening of the marital institution this has been slightly alleviated).[19] The declining momentum of the deteriorating phase of relationships is thus spurred to a slight final reversal (albeit negative) by the intensification required to cut the affective cord.

As contrasted with task achievement, where a lag effect was noted, the effort invested in affective relationships yields a nearly *simultaneous gratification*. In fact, the drive theory of arousal (Spence and Spence, 1966) seems the most suitable framework for analyzing the correspondence between stimulus and performance in this sphere: The quality of the communion varies directly and immediately with the attention, effort, and intensity conferred, only reaching a ceiling when the intangible maximum of human emotional output is reached.

CAREERS

Let us now examine the complex interweaving of multiple events and achievements that combine to constitute the momentum of an entire career. Here, the efforts of the individual are influenced by a multiplicity of other, larger factors that cojointly contribute to forging the progression of each person's career performance. Rising to importance in this arena of everyday life are the more structurally and temporarily macro elements of the social world.

Types of Ascent

Professions vary in the pace and tempo of their members' abilities to gain success and stature, some promoting an immediate rise to fortune and others demanding long toil before headway can be made. Remembering that there is always a flexibility and range of career movement, I will examine those professions displaying diverse patterns of ascension to peak momentum, drawing upon a general characterization of occupational structure and norms presented in each field.

A *rapid* rise to the top, epitomized in the extreme by the "instant hit," is found in pursuits that value talent as the main criterion for advancement. With effort, ability, and the ineluctable whimsies of luck, a person can forge ahead without delay, relatively unhampered by an institutionally necessitated period of apprenticeship. Sports fans regularly witness this phenomenon, where a rookie makes a splash during his first year in the league. The creative professions with popular appeal, from filmmaking to novel-writing to rock music, also illustrate this ideal typical, swift route to overnight stardom, as does revolutionary politics, where a charismatic leader can move from outcast to governor through a single coup d'etat. Once presented, any new achievement, regardless of the age of its inventor-constructor or the length of time he or she has previously spent in the profession, can launch its creator into a headlong upward momentum if it is well received. This is only possible, however, in loosely structured fields, unencumbered by either formal or informal controls, and permitting a continuous, fluid hierarchical rearrangement.

Another cluster of professions is commonly characterized by a more *moderate* rate of momentum's onset. Occupations such as academics, politics, small business, individual entrepreneurship, and the creative arts exhibit this form of career escalation. Here, talent remains important to success, but the volatile extremes of ascent are restrained by an established system of stratification that ensures a modicum of solidarity. Some combination of skill, knowledge, and experience is considered necessary to reach a career peak, but this can only be attained after a period of time spent rising through the ranks. Recognition, though, is not limited to this factor alone, but is granted in concert with proven ability. Thus, there is room for creative expression but it is qualified by informal norms of ascendance. While it is not mandatory to follow any specific pattern, certain steps naturally lead to others, the speed of movement depending on either innate talent or the formation of a set of friends, sponsors, or business connections that can promote personal prominence.[20] *Semistructured* best describes the degree of control modulating these occupations and shaping the career ascent of intermediate speed.

Trades whose members climb to the top at a uniformly *slow* rate contain the least dynamic fluctuations in momentum.

Heavily bureaucratized organizations riddled with ceremonious hierarchy and rank restrict individuals' careers to torpidity by structurally discouraging the launch of momentum. Government, military, and large industrial institutions are especially prone to such sluggish courses of professional advancement, with their formalized requirement dictating universal career ascent. Individual aspiration, effort, and initiative are often deadened in such circumstances, because superior performance is not rewarded with upward mobility (and greater pay) so much as inferior action that merely follows the normative pathway. The nadir of career escalation (representing total inertia) is being "frozen in rank, trapped on a seniority list waiting for one's superior to die or retire" (Lyman and Scott, 1970: 203). This results from the totally controlled and structured occupational environment.

Location of Peaking

Careers can also be analytically differentiated by their propensity to climax in momentum at varying stages along the "time track" (Lyman and Scott, 1970: 189-212). Ironically, as Berger (1979: 61-62) implies, the capture of momentum during a particular professional period may have less to do with the quality of one's production than with the serendipity of synchrony between a creation and its audience's receptivity. Still, certain occupations have inbred demand structures enhancing or negating momentum's potency according to intellectual, emotional, or physical limitations.

Callings that rely heavily on physical appearance, prowess, or conditioning promote *early* career summits. Athletes, models, and dancers, for example, enjoy great success and exposure during their twenties and early thirties, fading into "over-the-hill" or "old-man" status after that. In concert music, child prodigies have a similar way of "burning out" early (Mozart being one of the great exceptions). Occupations that emphasize precocity also expect and grant the fullest career rewards at a young age. Individuals in these fields (e.g., composers, conductors, gymnasts, and some natural scientists) must therefore establish themselves early for their potential to be recognized (Lyman and Scott, 1970: 198).[21] Further, many blue-collar occupations offer an advancement structure that features early momentum peaking. These trades are so limited in their range of escalation opportunities that people in such professions as plumbing and carpentry may attain the height of their momentum by the age of thirty and never advance further. Beyond the specific nature of particular occupational peculiarities, early peaking is fostered by a widespread societal preoccupation with youth. Cultures that favor the attributes of early life will be inclined to look highly on and grant greater respect to those in that cycle, aiding a generally advanced career momentum climax.

In pursuits placing a premium on maturity, *mid*-career performance zeniths obtain. Mastery of a complex subject matter may defer maximum efficiency and quality of achievement until middle-age or professional involvement is attained, as in leadership positions. By contrast, conferring total security at an intermediate stage (as in the academic tenure system) often stimulates a diminished productive velocity beyond that point. Once again, momentum's medial peaking locale is enhanced by society's evaluatory concurrence, according status and prominence to those in their forties and fifties. Modern American civilization illustrates this condition, having extended the youth barrier to nearly thirty, this being generally followed by a period of apprenticeship and experimentation. Aged persons are not highly respected either, as witnessed by mandatory retirement ages, the isolation of the elderly from their relatives, and loss of self-esteem and power among senior citizens.[22]

Late peaking can be found in metiers where the accumulation of wisdom, experience, and a broad net of associations is of foremost value. Religious roles, focusing on the venerated position of community elders and sagacious leaders (heightened where ancestor worship prevails), highlight the former aspect of contributing factors. Where peak achievement is rooted in escalation through a ladder system or the accumulation of connections, trades with a social foundation—such as charity fund-raising or those relying on established business influence, as in the idealized conception of organized-crime "godfathers"—come to the fore. Traditionalistic, paternalistic cultural milieux support a position of strength and power for time-honored leaders, businessmen, and citizens, favoring their later years as the mightiest ones, those most likely to demonstrate the fully aroused, profound, and productive spiraling pattern.

Duration and Quality of Peaks

Career momentum can vary from the intense but short-lived to the moderate but enduring, making anywhere from one appearance to several repeated showings. The *stability-fragility continuum* of permanence appears directly related to the degree and type of structural control governing an occupational setting: More regulated fields, where a slower course of ascension prevails, promote "placid" performance tenacity, while loosely flowing occupations characterized by rapid shoots to stardom yield a volatile, "explosive" achievement that can quickly dissipate. In the latter professions one must be constantly aware of one's momentum level, boosting it with freshly wrought impulses whenever it shows signs of weakening:

> Artists prize momentum. Having it means getting lots of exposure because of a hit record and a thriving tour. It is especially crucial to new artists or those who have been struggling for years with minimal success. . . . An artist maintains momentum by rapidly following a success with another. . . . In the first half of last year Stewart was in demand. Because of his first album, "Year of the Cat," and his first single, the album's title song, a six-week tour was stretched to seven months. To maintain momentum, Stewart would have had to come up with another album four or five months after the tour ended in August. But Stewart has been tardy. That followup album, "Time Passages," has just been released by his new label, Arista, exactly two years after "Year of the Cat" came out. . . . The cardinal sin, which

> Stewart committed, is allowing your career to cool off [Hunt, 1978: 1, 85].

This popular-music example shows that some members of that trade are aware of momentum's internal dynamics and how the timing of events can be crucial to following up on an impulse to achieve and sustain carry-through. Here we see that there is clearly more to career momentum than producing a quality product via methodical creative efforts. Synchronizing the vital elements of motion in an optimally coordinated fashion enables the performer to seize upon the breakdown of resistance force (professional recognition and receptivity) and the possession of prior impetus (success and popularity) to achieve the fully aligned, powerfully charging force that is momentum.

Serving as a foil to this volatile state is the relative security guaranteed by professions engineering more control over career fluctuation. By exerting a normalizing influence over occupational mobility, they can help to ensure that once a peak is attained, momentum can be maintained at a respectable plateau until retirement (and honorarily thereafter).

Multiple momentum peaks throughout the course of a career occur commonly, although they are rarely of equal intensity (like second winds). Not every invention is as brilliant as the last, and creative crests differ in kind from professional zeniths based on interpersonal connections. But, true to the continuum, the greatest number of separate momenta are found in the structurally unrestricted trades, descending in quantity as greater career guidelines appear.

Depending on the stage of one's career, one is motivated toward and reacts to pinnacles differently. In youth, the individual is known as "up and coming," "full of potential," and "promising." Having become experienced, he or she is referred to with phrases like "in the prime" and "well seasoned." Rebounding from a deteriorating state to score a peak is much harder; those in this category are dubiously honored as "retreads," "comebacks," and "final gasps." Such "last chances" stem from "either a steeled burst of emotional and physical control (e.g., when a tiring boxer prepares himself for the tenth round) or abandonment of causation and calculation and the taking of reckless risks (e.g., when soldiers, hopelessly outnumbered, charge their opponents)" (Lyman and Scott, 1970: 209). Beyond internal causation, multiple peaks result from the ebb and flow of fads and fashions, getting traded or rediscovered, and chance flukes.

Finales

A career with momentum may lose this inner motion either lingeringly or abruptly. *Leisurely* ends are often caused by evolutions in taste and technology, leaving an individual or a whole occupation descending into stale inertia ("a dying breed"). The decline may simply result from a slow abandonment of effort, where a conscious deceleration is tiredly accepted. "Petering out," in a gradual sense, can sometimes be associated with those who try to hang on "past their prime," extending professional involvement beyond the point where fresh impulses can be satisfactorily generated. By "dragging out" the decaying phase, people run the risk of incurring such a heavy negative momentum that it imposes on the memory of a previously sparkling career.

Sudden death, not uncommon to careers, strikes startlingly, bringing momentum to a precipitous end. Withdrawal can be temporary, due to a disabling injury, a setback, or the ubiquitous swing of fad and fashion. When permanent, voluntary retirement can prompt either the greatest or the least change in achievement level through the antipodal exultant desire to "quit while you're ahead" or the sheepish decision to retreat before causing further embarrassment to self and others. Forced retirement generally terminates the occupational progress of those who have attained average or lower-level momentum, as these are either "lifers" who have held on to jobs they execute adequately or "slackers" who are being fired. Of course, actual death strikes indiscriminately at all plateaus of intensity, bringing a final and complete conclusion to a lifetime of accomplishment.[23]

An overview of the relationship between momentum and career development suggests that *macrostructural* factors embedded in various occupational milieux have the greatest influence on the average performance intensity achieved. Tempo, dynamic forces, and freedom of progression are augmented in fluid, unrestricted fields, while they are restrained for those in jobs with increasing degrees of formal and informal (normative) control. At one extreme of this continuum we observe the impulse that meets so little hierarchical resistance that it instantaneously catapults its producer to fortune, only to lose velocity shortly thereafter, when it is replaced by another impetuous achievement by another person. The antithesis lies in callings so bureaucratically mechanized that advancement along the career path is pedantically mundane—movement robbed of all momentum.

CONCLUSION

This chapter has examined several different levels and types of activities, located in various spheres of life. We have seen how momentum occurs in both the micro and the macro realm(s), from the daily fluctuation possible in a relationship to the yearly fluctuation often taken by a career. We have also seen it display subtle transformations in character and sequence, depending on the situation and behavior in which it is lodged, yet throughout these adaptations it can be recognized as revealing a fundamental constancy of form, construction, feeling, and effect.

Momentum's capacity to boost performance, enhancing the quality and quantity of goal attainment, often places those possessing it in a favorable position. How others perceive those in this advantageous situation constitutes the *interrelations of momentum.* One responsive pose is affiliative, where friends and acquaintances admire achievers, taking warm pride in their success. Others equally propelled may be drawn to them as compatriots, to share the experience of their mutual feelings and force of intensity. Those in less fortunate circumstances may be attracted to their limelight, hoping to "ride their coattails" to a similar state of velocity or to absorb it through contagion. Concurrent with the placebo effect, this may occur regardless of whether real momentum has or has not been attained.

Rejoicing at others' exploits is not universal, however, and individuals with momentum may find many adopting a rejecting attitude. Filled with jealousy, they may retrench, steering clear of former colleagues or friends altogether. A jump to the extreme of outright hostility is generally restrained, though, by the curbing influence of microsocial norms, labeling this reaction as unacceptable.[24]

One of momentum's ironies is the *contrasting function* of several component factors and activities. As we learned from time-outs (Chapter 3) and the alternately channeling and disorganizing effect of emotions (Chapter 2), the same behavior can act as either a help or a hindrance to the growth of intensity under different circumstances. This repeatedly evident dual effect contributes to the necessity for understanding particularistic, situational details in order to make the final assessment about the influence any element will produce. The repetition of everyday life activities provides another illustrated case. People become accustomed to performing certain chores with the ritualization of daily regularity, using them to form a habitual framework for their lives that provides comfort and security. Such routinization can act as a barrier to momentum, for should an impulse arise and try to sweep to performance intensity, the repetition of daily rituals (such as reading the paper at a certain hour) serves as a flow breaker. In fact, the routinized nature of most life is an important cause of momentum's rarity.

Other circumstances foster repetition's role as a strengthening agent to momentum. As noted in task achievement, the regular recurrence of an activity can lead to accelerated motion through growing psychological and manual familiarity. Performance level can thus rise while attention is simultaneously liberated to focus on future planning, promoting further ease of accomplishment. Furthermore, repetitive daily rituals can also serve as momentum enhancers under different circumstances. People freed of all repetition may suddenly find themselves floating aimlessly, unable to develop a repetitive routine on which to start building the rhythm of momentum. Here, repetition is the key to fostering a complex, patterned flow. Thus, a single constituent can alternately provide the divergent effects of distraction and concentration, depending on the situated motivation, underlying meaning, and needs of the individuals involved.

A concluding remark concerns the role of structure and control (on both micro and macro levels) in influencing everyday life momentum. In the micro sphere, the behavioral norms of tact, etiquette, courtesy, and custom have certain positive effects on momentum. By cautioning against brash behavior that could ultimately lead to interactional faux pas and by alerting individuals to recognized symbols of mutual interest, informal social controls aid in the development of carefully planned performance. In a more retentive vein, momentum breakers are structurally avoided, especially when social values condemn them (as in divorce), urging the preservation of whatever force remains rather than starting anew. But hindrance is the far greater effect of such polite rules and regulations, because they rob life of its piquancy and zest, essential ingredients of the dynamic ascension to momentum. Their influence is fundamentally conservative, deterring spontaneity and risk-taking. Breaking out of day-to-day mundanity and rising to excelled performance often requires the ability boldly to thrust aside the dictates of society and create a charisma that will serve as a vehicle to the heights of intensity, velocity, and spirit.

Overviewing the momentum of a life span from a macro plane reveals a similar pattern. Institutional norms enhance momentum superficially by guaranteeing the stable endurance of performative crests in areas widely governed by structural foundations. Closer examination supports the opposite view, however, crediting large-scale organization with an inert influence. Dynamic fluctuation, a common result of uncontrolled entrepreneurial ventures, is practically eliminated, eradicating the sudden and powerful leap to success or failure. Initiative is denied by the combination of restrictions to advancement and guarantees against disappointment, often promoting incompetence through the Peter Principle (advancement to the level of inadequacy). Thus, life's dynamic potential for momentum development is generally inhibited by all forms of structural impingement and aided by a free-flowing atmosphere encouraging daring, creative expression.

NOTES

1. It is interesting to note that noradrenaline is cited as instrumental in regulating secretion of melatonin and hence the circadian fluctuation and its associated ebb and flow. This organic bodily chemical was also considered instrumental in the arousal process, physiologists ascribing it a role in heightening activation and preparedness to act or respond.

2. Research into the relationship between circadian rhythms and mental illness, manic depression, and schizophrenia is currently being conducted by clinical psychobiologists at the National Institute for Mental Health under the leadership of Dr. Fredrick K. Goodwin. A recent paper, presented at the 1978 American Psychological Association meetings (as described in Timnick, 1978), reports on their ability to influence mood variations by chemically manipulating the biological clocks of humans and animals.

3. Fiske and Maddi (1961) also correlate this with activation and arousal.

4. A plethora of studies have investigated and documented these circadian effects. They are too numerous to cite here; a good review can be found in Luce (1971: 8-11, 31-35).

5. Although this effect has been noted by many researchers, one particularly interesting experiment was reported by a French speleologist, Michel Siffre (Siffre et al., 1966), who spent a long period submerged in a cave. Despite his most careful efforts to keep track of the days, when Siffre emerged from underground at the end of what had seemed like thirty-five days, he discovered that two full months had elapsed.

6. Actually, biorhythm theory was first advanced in the late nineteenth century in Europe. Studies concluded that the physical, emotional, and intellectual states of humans fluctuate rhythmically. Currently, theorists believe that these three cycles move unvaryingly through an individual's lifetime. The physical cycle is said to last 23 days, the emotional 28 days, and the intellectual 33 days. For a more detailed review, see Amdur (1977), Louis (1978), and Parlee (1978).

7. See Luce (1971: 25). While such an undertaking would be an awesomely mammoth task, it would at least serve to sensitize the observer to the existence and importance of everyday life's very potent ebb and flow.

8. Mead (1938) refers to this stage of the act as "impulse": the visceral thrust to performance.

9. Mead considers this the "perception" stage of the act, where the individual internalizes the planned desired behavior. Further, this "percept" is equivalent to the collapsed act, where the full range of sensations that will ultimately arise from it are telescoped and experienced in anticipation.

10. "Manipulation" marks Mead's conception of the third stage's origin, which endures through the final portion of industrious activity.

11. At this point Mead's final stage of the act, "consummation," occurs, where the individual psychologically reviews the entire course of action and forms an appraisal of its worth.

12. In addition, should another project be immediately undertaken, the level of velocity still inherent would enable the individual to accelerate through its early stages with ease.

13. See Lyman and Scott (1970: 194) for an introduction to the continuous-episodic dimension in time tracks generally.

14. Deemed by many the turning point in a relationship, this significant event can vary from conversational intimacy (confessions of deep or past feelings) to physical sealing (a memorable, lingering kiss) or interactional aid (support during an outside crisis).

15. See Lyman and Scott (1970: 195-196). It is also interesting to note that in popular folklore a measure of one's sexual openness or permissiveness is often couched in terms of velocity, ranging from "fast" to "slow."

16. Also noted by Davis (1973: 209-245) as "have it outs" and "work it outs."

17. Most affairs, either between singles or adulterous persons, end here, as the passionate excitation of challenge, strangeness, and discovery withers.

18. Fiske and Maddi (1961) posit that arousal diminishes in the organism as relative novelty wears off.

19. One informant who had just completed an amicable divorce from her husband and was still dating him reported terrible social condemnation, friends asserting that if they still liked each other so much they should have tried harder to save the marriage.

20. Kadushin (1976) and Peterson and White (1979: 414) particularly note the importance of professional social *circles* to painters, writers, and poets, whose acclaim may be more a function of the company they keep (which takes time to develop) than the quality of the works of art they produce.

21. One closely related exception to this trend is the case of classical music virtuousi, who usually mature as artists over reasonably long periods of time.

22. For more detailed descriptions of the state of the elderly in our society, see especially Cowgill and Holmes (1972), Rosow (1974) and Fontana (1977).

23. Ironically, in some cases this can spark a posthumous career momentum, especially for creative artists whose productive capacity is now definitely limited.

24. The whole notion of "interrelations of momentum" represents a human counterpart to Descartes' discussion of collisions between inanimate objects. When people display affiliative behavior they are following the adhesive model of contact, but when they react rejectively they manifest elastic or explosive momentum.

6

CONCLUSION

The purpose of this work has been to create a theory of momentum, to provide insights into its internal and external construction, and then to show how these abstract notions manifest themselves in the social world. The theory I offer is a dynamic one, taking an active view of human nature and addressing an active facet of human life. While the focus I bring to bear is grounded in existential and absurdist sociology's emphasis on the importance of subjective perceptions and the constructed nature of social meanings and understandings, I also feel that some form of reality exists "out there" which provides a basis for those perceptions and meanings. Thus, in this analysis, I am concerned with both the behavioral forms that produce momentum and the way these do or do not become socially perceived, interpreted, and evaluated.

Momentum rises above most active endeavors as an elite form of behavior, one graced by a heightened progression toward the goal and one which fills its possessors with an infectiously uplifting feeling of special accomplishment and ability. In Chapters 1 and 2 I presented a definition of momentum, outlining its diverse types and styles, the components that constitute it, its sequential unfolding process and a range of its characteristics. Whether positive or negative, explosive or placid, fleeting or enduring, momentum signifies a certain mode of action that is situationally flexible, yet rooted in an underlying constancy of form. Not every acceleration achieves this status, despite its creation of positive or negative motion. Instead, the term is reserved for those instances where the full complement of elements merge into the proper synchronization. Momentum's wax and wane, as distinct from the wax and wane of ordinary existence, is thus marked by *a sense of direction; an initial (primitive) impetus; a sophisticated carry-through process encompassing the circular return (feedback) of expended energy through the satisfaction obtained from previous efforts and the anticipation of future gratification; an internally self-generating feature combining continuing fresh impulses with this recycled derivative impulse; and a repetitive internal form whereby people continuously pass through the stages of motivation, emotion, arousal, action, and feedback to create the spiral of intensification that builds positive or negative force.*

Chapters 3, 4, and 5 then provide the empirical arenas where this theory of momentum is examined in operation. From the micro realm of sport to the broad-ranging expanse of the stock market to the generically grouped everyday life activities considered, we witnessed momentum's characteristic stamp on all the actions it touched. We also saw that people are more attuned to noticing momentum in areas where they come to expect its presence (like sport and the stock market), ignoring its effects at other times (as often happens in task achievement). People's reactions to the perception of momentum can vary even further. In some cases people react affiliatively, being favorably drawn to those they think have momentum, while at other times they competitively reject those whom they believe possess this powerful moving force.

CONTRIBUTIONS

By elucidating the characteristics and dimensions of momentum's sociological nature, the advancement of scientific knowledge has been served in several ways. The first lies in the *processual nature of the analysis* I have offered. In sociology, humans and their deeds are too often portrayed as static, atemporal abstractions forming segments of structural, societal designs. My theory of social action is contrastingly dynamic, concentrating on the vibrant processes within these institutional boundaries that constitute the actual fiber of human existence. Thus, instead of providing the reader with a snapshot image that illustrates details of a frozen and extracted slice of life, I have tried to capture the fullness of a cinema, experiencing vitality as projected by a motion picture camera.

Through this means I have also sought to illuminate *momentum's complex inner nature*, elucidating its more trenchant characteristics and their interrelations. A dynamic spiraling force, it requires the full complement and synchronization of componential subsystems in order to be realized. One must, then, admire the potential of human nature even more, for despite its complexity, momentum is a naturally occurring form of human behavior: It need not be orchestrated to arise.

Momentum's social nature constitutes another facet of its existence: that involving its subjective perception, framing, and construction. Whether or not momentum is actually attained through the proper spiraling alignment of component characteristics is not a concern on this level; that issue is relevant only to the unconscious and objective dimension of human life. In fact, momentum's presence can go unnoticed, passing as nothing more than the apex of an ebb or flow, not especially distinguished from the ordinary rhythms of daily life. But when behavior is recognized as momentum-infused, it receives an extra boost capable of propelling it to higher planes. This comes from people consciously reacting to it and according it the symbolic significance of a special dynamic capable of generating great force. Here momentum gains a social reality for those experiencing it and surrounding others. Its meaning is created and framed through the process of social interaction, which often sets the tone for whether people will react affiliatively or rejectively and whether the momentum will become highly infectious or remain socially contained. It can thus vary greatly in nature according to how it is perceived, interpreted, and evaluated by individuals and groups.

These two dimensions of momentum's nature should not be viewed as at odds with each other or mutually exclusive; rather, they exist cojointly and are mutually influential. As I noted at the beginning of this chapter, concrete forms of reality do provide the foundation on which social meanings are constructed, while collective beliefs can have very real effects on the evolution of tangible acts and situations. Hence, we study them both to learn more about the relation between these two spheres.

The insights revealed in this study have the potential to *change one's perception of the world*, to offer the reader a new glimmer of awareness into the workings of human behavior. A theory of social action, these perceptions, conceptions, and models of momentum highlight the intensity, flow, rhythm, and progress of human life. Too often the dynamics of existence are overlooked or misunderstood by people who focus their attention on structures, settings, and isolated events. This work suggests that people look not only at the societal structures and specific activities taking place within them, but also at the form and flow of those actions. Thus, life can be viewed as a procession of unfolding developments that fluctuate in thrust, pace, capacity for growth, and degree of propulsive force. By developing their knowledge of momentum and its characteristics, social analysts and everyday actors can gain familiarity with varying stages in the rise and fall of the momentum sequence and learn to recognize potential momentum contributors and breakers. In this way, they can effect a slight shift in their perception of social action, attaining a "momentum perspective on the world"—a cultivated sensitivity to instances of momentum's possibility, its attainment, and elements fostering its elongation, enhancement, or diminishment.

Practical utility can also result from this knowledge: Recognizing those correlates associated with performance escalation, people can intentionally strive to attain them rather than ineffectually groping for accelerated intensity in self-negating ways. Specifically, people can reevaluate their social and psychological approach to an activity, trying to find areas of inner contradiction, lack of concentration, distracting or competing side motivation, or poor social organization that can weaken their potential for effort and accomplishment. Groups unable to generate momentum may want to shift their focus, striving for new stimulation that could provide greater relative novelty and arousal, or they may want to shift their goals, changing from striving for maximal performance in all areas to concentrating on achieving success in first one and later other areas. Concomitantly, awareness of potential momentum breakers and their role helps people avoid the unfortunate loss of a streaming flow so excruciatingly built. Here, sensitivity to appropriate interruption points is particularly important. As we have seen, the greatest damage to momentum occurs when the rhythm of work or play is broken during periods of peaking. By building in the flexibility to extend temporal involvement with projects when progress really picks up, one can capitalize on the existing dynamic power of these times and reap greater rewards from a constant amount of effort. Stopping work at natural break points is an improvement, but then one often returns to a task at the nadir of involvement with the subject. Since getting started is the most difficult aspect of any endeavor, continuing to work past the natural break point through the next introductory build-up phase once again capitalizes on the momentum that has been generated. After the period of rest, the return to work is facilitated because a start has already been made and the direction of the day's efforts partly determined.

APPLICABILITY

The groundwork laid here is fertile in potential applicability to new fields and directions. The theory I have offered is intended to serve as a springboard for further investigation of both momentum's multifaceted character and other spheres of life it touches. It is my hope that momentum, long an important variable in the physical sciences, can thus be developed into a viable research tool for the analysis of social behavior.

As I noted in Chapter 1, implications of momentum theory stand in short-range contradiction to a common scientific and folk maxim: the law of averages. Often referred to in sport as "dueness," we can note the general cultural expectation of this principle in the game of baseball. Here, the greatest offensive danger is often anticipated from the high-batting-average player who has yet to score a hit by the late innings of the game, based on the notion that players who have hit repeatedly may have used up all their potential power for that game. Momentum theory, however, postulates that in cases where this dynamic, spiraling force has been achieved, like behavior will be followed by like. A batter on a hot streak would thus be the pitcher's most fearsome challenge, not the ordinary good player who is temporarily in a slump. While the law of averages (embodying elements connoted by the notion of fate) may or may not obtain among humans in the long run, this study of behavioral dynamics suggests that it is invalid in the short run, and that the opposite does, in fact, hold true. Thus, momentum theory rejects any short-term predicting that is based on averaging principles and supports anticipations rooted in the view of behavior as charged with vigorous trends and swings.

Another behavioral sphere to which momentum theory adds insight is psychology's conception of arousal. Here, the debate over optimal levels of arousal between proponents of drive theory and proponents of the inverted-U hypothesis could be augmented by what we have learned from studying momentum. A "natural ceiling" model of arousal is suggested by the present study, where performance and/or intensity rises directly, up to a certain point (the apex of the inverted-U). Increased negative forms of arousal, such as pressure, would cause performance to diminish, as inverted-U hypothesists suggest; but increased positive forms of arousal, such as the pleasure generated by a romantic relationship, would cause performance to continue at the "natural ceiling" level for as long as the arousal remains constant or escalating.

Third, collective behavior theory can also be seen to overlap with momentum theory in the area of behavioral contagion. As collective beliefs or movements arise and begin to spread in acceptance and force, they cojointly draw on the interpersonal dynamics of groups and the escalating intensity found in the momentum spiral. These two bodies of theory can also aid our understanding of each other; The "contagion of momentum" explains how momentum is transmitted from person to person and the "momentum of contagion" illustrates how the expansion of imitative behavior can fluctuate in strength and power according to a certain sequence.

Insights generated from momentum theory can also be applied to many other areas, too numerous to discuss in detail here. Schatzman (in Glaser and Strauss, 1967: 40) has suggested, for example, that the conceptualization process in field research displays momentum, as the first formulating of ideas is usually followed by an onslaught of subsequent ones that snowball and grow excitingly. On a more macro level, social movements, politics, and societal evolution appear to display the dynamic characteristics of momentum. Subjects encompassing processual evolution, movement, or reaction are hence particularly susceptible to momentum's influence and are worth investigating along this dimension.

Finally, momentum can be applied as a concrete variable in ways other than I have done here, through various methodological approaches and theoretical paradigms. Augmenting the comprehensiveness of this research, momentum can advantageously be scrutinized by experimental social scientists. Emphasizing a whole new range of foci and ramifications, experimental researchers might attempt to evaluate, verify, modify, or disprove parts of the theory I have proposed. Researchers preferring a macrostructural approach can make further use of momentum in examining institutions, societies, and historical movements. Finally, microinteractional sociologists can expand on my work in a similar vein, considering other uninvestigated types of behavior and areas of life (for example, the idea of "social chemistry").

Admittedly, I have only scratched the surface. Much more can be learned about this topic. My purpose throughout has been to elevate for consideration this heretofore neglected sociological dimension and to provide social scientists with a new analytical tool. The intended value of this work lies not only in the theory I have proposed, but beyond it, to the underlying questions implicitly raised about the vicissitudes of motion interpenetrating the core of human social existence.

REFERENCES

Adler, Patricia A. and Peter Adler (1980) "The social psychology of the stock market." Presented at the annual meetings of the American Sociological Association, New York.

Adler, Peter and Patricia A. Adler (1978) "The role of momentum in sport." *Urban Life* 7, 2.

Alexander, Sidney S., (1961) "Price movements in speculative markets: trends or random walks." *Industrial Management Review* (May).

Amdur, Neil (1977) "The 12th man in the huddle: a biorhythm expert." *New York Times Sunday Sports* (December 4).

Ardrey, Robert (1968) *The Territorial Imperative.* New York: Atheneum.

Astrand, Per-Olof and Kaare Rodahl (1977) *Textbook of Work Physiology.* New York: McGraw-Hill.

Atkinson, John W. (1964) *An Introduction to Motivation.* New York: Litton.

——— (1968) "Achievement motivation," in David Shils (ed.) *International Encyclopedia of the Social Sciences,* Volume 1. New York: Macmillan.

Ball, Donald W. (1973) "The biological bases of human society," in Jack D. Douglas (ed.) *Introduction to Sociology.* New York: Free Press.

Baumol, William J. (1965) *The Stock Market and Economic Efficiency.* New York: Fordham University Press.

Berger, Bennett M. (1979) "Two cheers for sociology." *Contemporary Sociology* 8, 1.

Bindra, Dalbir (1968) "Neuropsychological interpretation of the effects of drive and incentive-motivation on general activity and instrumental behavior," *Psychological Review* 75, 1.

Blumer, Herbert (1951) "Collective behavior," pp. 161-222 in A. M. Lee (ed.) *New Outline of the Principles of Sociology.* New York: Barnes & Noble.

Bond, Frederic D. (1930) *Stock Movements and Speculation.* Englewood Cliffs, NJ: Prentice-Hall.

Bouton, Jim (1970) *Ball Four.* New York: Dell.

Bradley, Bill (1976) *Life on the Run.* New York: Quadrangle.

Cannon, Walter B. (1929) *Bodily Changes in Pain, Hunger, Fear and Rage.* Boston: Bradford.

Cohen, Jerry (1977) "Superstars: how it feels to triumph." *Los Angeles Times* (January 30).

Cook, M. B. and M. S. Pembry (1913) "Observations on the effect of muscular exercise upon man." *English Journal of Physiology* 45.

Cootner, Paul [ed.] (1964) *The Random Character of Stock Market Prices.* Cambridge, MA: MIT Press.

Couch, Carl (1970) "Dimensions of association in collective behavior episodes." *Sociometry* 33, 4.
Cowgill, Donald and Lowel Holmes [eds.] (1972) *Aging and Modernization*. Englewood Cliffs, NJ: Prentice-Hall.
Davis, Murray S. (1973) *Intimate Relations*. New York: Free Press.
DeVore, Irven [ed.] (1965) *Primate Behavior: Field Studies on Monkeys and Apes*. New York: Holt, Rinehart & Winston.
Douglas, Jack (1971) *American Social Order* New York: Free Press.
Douglas, Jack D. and John M. Johnson [eds.] (1977) *Existential Sociology*, New York: Cambridge University Press.
Dreman, David N. (1977) *Psychology and The Stock Market*. New York: Amacom.
Easterbrook, J. A. (1959) "The effect of emotion on cue utilization and the organization of behavior." *Psychological Review* 66.
Faulkner, Robert R. (1976) "Making violence by doing work: selves, situations and the world of professional hockey," in David M. Landers (ed.) *Social Problems in Athletics*. Urbana: University of Illinois Press.
Feather, Norman T. (1961) "The relationship of persistence at a task to expectation of success and achievement related motives." *Journal of Abnormal and Social Psychology* 63.
Festinger, L., A. Pepitone, and T. Newcombe (1953) "Some consequences of de-individuation on a group." *Journal of Abnormal and Social Psychology* 47.
Fiske, Donald W. and Salvatore R. Maddi [eds.] (1961) *Functions of Varied Experience*. Homewood, IL: Irwin.
Fontana, Andrea (1977) *The Last Frontier*. Beverly Hills, CA: Sage.
Frank, Jerome (1961) *Persuasion and Healing: A Comparative Study of Psychotherapy*. Baltimore: Johns Hopkins University Press.
Freeman, G. L. (1948) *The Energetics of Human Behavior*. Ithaca, NY: Cornell University Press.
Freud, Sigmund (1922) Group Psychology and the Analysis of the Ego. New York: Liveright.
——— (1948) *Beyond the Pleasure Principle*. London: Hogarth.
Furlong, William B. (1976) "Baseball's designated jitters." *T.V. Guide* 24, 42.
Gabbey, Alan (1971) "Force and inertia in seventeenth-century dynamics." *Studies of History and Philosophy of Science* 2, 1.
Glaser, Barney G. and Anselm L. Strauss (1967) *The Discovery of Grounded Theory*. Chicago: AVC.
Gmelch, George (1972) "Magic in professional baseball," in Gregory Stone (ed.) *Games, Sport and Power*. New Brunswick, NJ: Transaction.
Goffman, Erving (1955) "On face work." *Psychiatry* 18 (August).
——— (1959) *The Presentation of Self in Everyday Life*, Garden City, NY: Doubleday Anchor.
——— (1961) *Encounters*. Indianapolis: Bobbs-Merrill.
——— (1963) *Behavior in Public Places*. New York: Free Press.
——— (1967) *Interaction Ritual*, Garden City, NY: Doubleday Anchor.
——— (1971) *Relations in Public*. New York: Haper & Row.
Golenbock, Peter (1975) *Dynasty*. Englewood Cliffs, NJ: Prentice-Hall.
Goodall, Jane (1965) "Chimpanzees of the Combe Street Reserve," in Irven DeVore (ed.) *Primate Behavior: Field Studies on Monkeys and Apes*. New York: Holt, Rinehart & Winston.

Granger, C.W.J. and O. Morgenstern (1963) "Spectral analysis of New York stock market prices." *Kyklos.*

——— (1970) *Predictability of Stock Market Prices.* Lexington, MA: D.C. Heath.

Green, Ted (1977) "Abdul-Jabbar is up and takes Lakers with him." *Los Angeles Times* (Sports Section).

Greer, Thom (1977) "Celtic Pride cited for team's success." *Los Angeles Times* (May 26): Sports Section.

Hall, K.R.L. and Irven DeVore (1965) "Baboon social behavior," in Irven DeVore (ed.) *Primate Behavior: Field Research on Monkeys and Apes.* New York: Holt, Rinehart & Winston.

Hayes, Samuel P. (1950) "Some psychological problems of economics." *Psychological Bulletin* 47, 4.

Hebb, D.O. (1955) "Drives and the CNS." *Psychological Review* 62.

Herrigel, Eugen (1953) *Zen in the Art of Archery.* New York: Pantheon.

Hull, Clark L. (1932) "The goal gradient hypothesis and maze learning." *Psychological Review* 39.

——— (1943) *Principles of Behavior.* Englewood Cliffs, NJ: Prentice-Hall.

Hunt, Dennis (1978) " 'Momentum is no worry'—Stewart." *Los Angeles Times Calendar* (September 24).

Hutchinson, T. W. (1938) *The Significance and Basic Postulates of Economic Theory.* London: MacMillan.

Jacobsen, Steve (1978) "Momentum: the heady part of sports." *Toronto Star* (January 29).

James, William (1890) Principles of Psychology, Volumes I, II. New York: Holt, Rinehart & Winston.

——— (1970) "The social self," in Gregory Stone and Harvey Farberman (eds.) *Social Psychology Through Symbolic Interaction.* Waltham, MA: Xerox.

Janis, Irving L. (1972) *Victims of Groupthink.* Boston: Houghton-Mifflin.

Jokl, Ernst (1964) *Physiology of Exercise.* Springfield, IL: Charles C Thomas.

Kadushin, Charles (1976) "Networks and circles in the production of culture," In R. A. Peterson (ed.) *The Production of Culture.* Beverly Hills, CA: Sage.

Katz, Elihu and Paul F. Lazarsfeld (1955) *Personal influence.* New York: Free Press.

Lauck, Dan (1978) "Winning through imagination." *Mainliner* (March).

Lawther, John D. (1972) *Sport Psychology.* Englewood Cliffs, NJ: Prentice-Hall.

Le Bon, Gustav (1897) *The Crowd.* New York: Macmillan.

Lever, Janet (1972) "Soccer as a Brazilian way of life," in Gregory Stone (ed.) *Games, Sport and Power.* New Brunswick, NJ: Transaction.

Lewin, Kurt (1935) *A Dynamic Theory of Personality.* New York: McGraw-Hill.

Little, Roger W. (1948) "Buddy relations and combat performance," in Morris Janowitz (ed.) *The New Military.* New York: Russell Sage.

Lorie, James H. and Mary T. Hamilton (1973) *The Stock Market: Theories and Evidence.* Homewood, IL: Irwin.

Los Angeles Times (1976a) "Morning brief." April 5: Sports Section.

——— (1976b) "Detroit's going wild over Fidrych." June 30: Sports Section.

——— (1978) "Emotional edge can be fleeting thing." October 17: Sports Section.

Louis, Arthur (1978) "Should you buy biorhythms?" *Psychology Today* (April).

Luce, Gay Gaer (1971) *Body Time.* New York: Pantheon.

Lyman, Stanford and Marvin B. Scott (1970) *A Sociology of the Absurd.* Santa Monica, CA: Goodyear.

Mackay, Charles (1932) *Extraordinary Popular Delusions and the Madness of Crowds.* New York: Noonday.

Malinowski, Bronislaw (1948) *Magic, Science and Religion.* New York: Doubleday.

Malkiel, Burton G. (1973) *A Random Walk Down Wall Street.* New York: Norton.

Malmo, R. B. (1959) "Activation: a nuerophysiological dimension." *Psychological Bulletin* 66.

Mandler, George (1975) *Mind and Emotion.* New York: John Wiley.

March, Robert H. (1970) *Physics for Poets.* New York: McGraw-Hill.

Martens, Rainer (1974) "Arousal and motor performance," in Jack H. Wilmore (ed.) *Exercise and Sport Sciences Review.* New York: Academic.

Maslow, Abraham (1943) "A theory of human motivation." *Psychological Review* 50.

Maslow, Jonathon (1978) "All psyched up." *Mainliner* (March).

Mayer, Kurt (1949) "Toward understanding economic behavior." *American Journal of Economics and Sociology* 8 (July).

McClelland, David C. (1961) *The Achieving Society.* New York: Litton.

McCurdy, James H. and Leonard A. Larson (1939) *The Physiology of Exercise.* Philadelphia: Lea & Febinger.

McDougall, W. (1910) *Introduction to Social Psychology.* Boston: Luce.

——— (1920) *The Group Mind.* New York: G. P. Putnam.

——— (1923) Outline of Psychology. New York: Scribners.

Mead, George H. (1932) *The Philosophy of the Present.* Chicago: Open Court.

——— (1934) *Mind, Self and Society.* Chicago: University of Chicago Press.

——— (1938) *The Philosophy of the Act.* Chicago: University of Chicago Press.

Merton, Robert K. (1968) "The self-fulfilling prophecy," in Robert K. Merton, *Social Theory and Social Structure.* New York: Free Press.

Moskos, Charles C. (1970) *The American Enlisted Man.* New York: Russell Sage.

Murphy, Robert F. (1960) *Headhunter's Heritage.* Berkeley: University of California Press.

Murray, Jim (1976) "No place like . . ." *Los Angeles Times,* (March 18): Sports Section.

Natanson, Maurice (1956) *The Social Dynamics of George H. Mead.* Washington, DC: Public Affairs Press.

Neill, Humphrey B. (1963) *The Art of Contrary Thinking.* New York: Caxton.

Novak, Michael (1976) *The Joy of Sports.* New York: Basic Books.

Park, Robert (1972) *The Crowd and the Public.* Chicago: University of Chicago Press.

——— and E. Burgess (1921) *Introduction to the Science of Sociology.* Chicago: University of Chicago Press.

Parlee, Mary Brown (1978) "The rhythm in man's lives." *Psychology Today* (April).

Pearman, William A. (1976) "The structure of sports as a determinant of player interaction." Presented at annual meetings of the American Sociological Association, New York.

Pepitone, Joe [with Berry Stainback] (1975) *Joe, You Coulda Made Us Proud.* New York: Dell.

Peterson, Richard A. and Howard G. White (1979) "The simplex located in art worlds." *Urban Life* 7, 4.

Piaget, Jean (1966) "Time perception in children," in J. T. Frazier (ed.) *The Voices of Time.* New York: Braziller.

Polsky, Ned (1967) *Hustlers, Beats and Others.* Chicago: AVC.

Portman, Adolph (1961) *Animals as Social Beings.* New York: Viking.

Pratt, Sereno S. (1912) *The Work of Wall Street.* Englewood Cliffs, NJ: Prentice-Hall.

Radcliffe-Brown, A. R. (1952) *Structure and Function in Primitive Society*. London: Oxford University Press.
Rappaport, Roy (1966) "Ritual in the ecology of a New Guinea people: an anthropological study of the Tsembaga Maring." Doctoral dissertation, Columbia University, Ann Arbor, Michigan. (University Microfilm)
Rasmussen, Paul and Kathleen J. Ferraro (n.d.) "Divorce: the process of dissolutionment." (unpublished)
Rolo, Charles J. and George J. Nelson [eds.] (1967) *The Anatomy of Wall Street*. Philadelphia: J. B. Lippincott.
Rose, Arnold M. (1951) "Rumor and the stock market." *Public Opinion Quarterly* 15 (Fall).
——— (1966) "A social psychological approach to the study of the stock market." *Kyklos* 19.
Ross, E. A. (1905) *Foundations of Sociology*. New York: Macmillan.
Rosow, Irving (1974) *Socialization to Old Age*. Berkeley: University of California Press.
Roth, Julius A. (1963) *Timetables*. Indianapolis: Bobbs-Merrill.
Russell, Bill and Taylor Branch (1979) *The Second Wind: Memoirs of an Opinionated Man*. New York: Random House.
Samuelson, Paul A. (1965) "Proof that properly anticipated prices fluctuate randomly." *Industrial Management Review* (Spring).
Santayana, Geooge (1922) *Soliloquies in England and Later Soliloquies*. New York: Scribners.
Schutz, Alfred (1967) *The Phenomenology of the Social World*. Evanston: Northwestern University Press.
Schwartz, Barry and Stephen F. Barsky (1977) "The home advantage." *Social Forces* 55, 3.
Scott, Marvin (1968) *The Racing Game*. Chicago: AVC.
Shibutani, Tamotsu (1968) "A cybernetic approach to motivation," in Walter Buckley (ed.) *Modern Systems Research for the Behavioral Scientist*. Chicago: AVC.
——— (1978) *The Derelicts of Company K*. Berkeley: University of California Press.
Shils, Edward A. and Morris Janowitz (1948) "Cohesion and disintegration in the Wehrmacht in World War II." *Public Opinion Quarterly* 12 (Summer).
Siffre, M. et al. (1966) "Studies on two healthy human subjects isolated for several months underground." *La Presse Medicale* 74.
Smelser, Neil (1962) *Theory of Collective Behavior*. New York: Free Press.
Smith, Adam (1967) *The Money Game*. New York: Random House.
Sorokin, Ptirim and Robert Merton (1937) "Social time: a methodological and functional analysis." *American Journal of Sociology* 42 (March): 615-629.
Spence, J. T. and K. W. Spence (1966) "The motivational components of manifest anxiety: drive and drive stimuli," in C. D. Spielberger (ed.) *Anxiety and Behavior*. New York: Academic.
Tarde, G. (1901) L'Opinion et la Foule. Paris: Alcan.
——— (1903) *The Laws of Imitation* (trans. E. C. Parsons). New York: Holt, Rinehart & Winston. (originally published 1890)
Thurlow, Bradbury K. (1967) "Contrary opinion theory: the psychological approach," in Charles J. Rolo and George J. Nelson (eds.) *The Anatomy of Wall Street*. Philadelphia: J. B. Lippincott.
Timnick, Lois (1978) "Body rhythms may be linked to illness." *Los Angeles Times* (October 10): Part 2.

Turner, Ralph H. and L. M. Killian (1972) *Collective Behavior.* Englewood Cliffs, NJ: Prentice-Hall.

Tutko, Thomas and Umberto Tosi (1976) *Sports Psyching.* Los Angeles: J. P. Tarcher.

Veroff, Joseph et al. (n.d.) "The use of thematic apperception to assess motivation in a nationwide interview study." Psychological Monograph 74, 12.

——— (1962) "Achievement motivation and religious background." *American Sociological Review* 27.

Watkins, Mel (1978) "Why N.B.A. teams succeed at home." *New York Times* (January 30).

Weiner, Philip P. [ed.] (1951) *Leibniz: Selections.* New York: Scribner.

Weiss, Paul (1969) *Sport: A Philosophic Inquiry.* Carbondale, IL: Southern Illinois University Press.

Wolff, Kurt H. [ed.] (1950) *The Sociology of Georg Simmel.* New York: Free Press.

Womack, Mari (1978) "Sports Magic." *Human Behavior* 7, 9.

Wooden, John [with Jack Tobin] (1972) *They Call Me Coach.* New York: Bantam.

Wright, Sam (1978) *Crowds and Riots.* Beverly Hills, CA: Sage.

Wyckoff, Peter (1963) *The Psychology of Stock Market Timing.* Englewood Cliffs, NJ: Prentice-Hall.

Wynne-Edwards, V. C. (1962) *Animal Dispersion in Relation to Social Behavior.* London: Oliver & Boyd.

Yerkes, R. M. and J. D. Dodson (1908) "The relation of strength of stimulus to rapidity of habit-formation." *Journal of Comparative Neurological Psychology* 18.

Zajonc, Robert B. (1965) "Social facilitation." *Science* 149.

Zurcher, Louis A. (1980) "The staging of emotion: a dramaturgical analysis." University of Texas, School of Social Work. (unpublished)

About the Author

Peter Adler is Assistant Professor of Sociology at the University of Tulsa. He received an A.B. degree from Washington University, an M.A. from the University of Chicago, and his Ph.D. from the University of California, San Diego. He has published essays on symbolic interactionism, drug use, and sport. His present research interests include art crimes, "beginners' luck," alcohol use, and the stock market.